How to Get Hired as a Scrum Master

FROM JOB ADS TO YOUR TRIAL DAY: LEARN HOW TO PICK THE RIGHT CLIENT OR EMPLOYER

STEFAN WOLPERS

Berlin Product People GmbH
Berlin, Germany

Imprint

© 2018 Berlin Product People GmbH, Berlin. (E-book version 1.0 on January 9th, 2018.)

Address: Berlin Product People GmbH, Borsigstrasse 8, 10115 Berlin, Germany.

Registered at: AG Charlottenburg (HRB 160341 B), Managing Director: Karl Wolpers.

Contact information: stefan.wolpers@berlin-product-people.com

All rights reserved. This, in particular, applies to the right to reproduce this book in a mechanical, electronic or photographic way, as well as storing and processing this book and its content in electronic systems of all kinds. It also applies to reprints of this book or parts of its content in magazines or newspapers or its utilization in whatever form on radio, TV or video, and its translation into other languages.

This book and its content were carefully researched and written. However, neither the author nor the publisher accepts any responsibility for the accuracy of its content or possible production errors such as typos.

Contents

Who Should Read This Book? — v
Prologue — Why This Book Was Written — vii
About the Author Stefan Wolpers — viii

PART I. THE JOB MARKET FOR SCRUM MASTERS AND AGILE COACHES

The Job Market Is Red Hot — 3
The Scrum Master Salary Report 2017 — 7

PART II. RESEARCH: HOW TO GET AN IDEA OF AN ORGANIZATION'S AGILE MATURITY

Proactive Research — 13
Analyzing a Job Advertisement — 23
Preparing for a Job Interview — 29

PART III. THE INTERVIEW: 47 SCRUM MASTER INTERVIEW QUESTIONS

Set 1: The Role of the Scrum Master — 39
Set 2: Backlog Refinement and Estimation — 51

Set 3: Sprint Planning	59
Set 4: Standups	69
Set 5: Retrospectives	77
Set 6: Agile Metrics	85
Set 7: How to Kick-off a Transition to Scrum	93
Set 8: Scrum Anti-Patterns	99
Conclusion (Advice for the Hiring Organization)	105

PART IV. THE TRIAL DAY: CHECKING THE CHEMISTRY

Preparing for Your Trial Day	109
Getting Started on Trial Day	117
Meet the Team and Get up to Speed	125
Possible Exercises During a Trial Day	131
Participating in Scrum Ceremonies	141
Less Suitable Topics for a Trial Day	183
Wrap-up Session at the End of a Trial Day	187

PART V. APPENDIX

What is Next?	191
Please Review the Book and Help Your Peers to Find it!	193
How to Get in Touch With Me	195
Other Books for Agile Practitioners	197

Who Should Read This Book?

No matter, if you are a product manager, a former engineer or a project manager: if you are looking to change your career and become a scrum master or agile coach this book will help you land a meaningful position.

Becoming "agile" is nowadays on the top of the agenda of many C-level executives. Their world is dominated by a paradigm shift, by the thought that software is eating the world, and that the speed of innovation is ever increasing. Probably, a startup has already been founded that will disrupt their business in a few years.

Hence, becoming "agile"— even when most organizations do not have an understanding what this means — is so crucial at the moment. And to do so, you will need to hire scrum masters and agile coaches, a trend that provides numerous job opportunities.

"How to Get Hired as a Scrum Master" is a hands-on guide for everyone interested in finding a suitable position as a scrum master or agile coach at an organization that already is agile or at least has a chance of adopting an agile mindset successfully over time.

The book covers all three phases that a candidate faces:

1. Identifying a suitable employer or client. (The principles of this book are equally applicable for freelancers.)
2. Preparing for and passing the job interview.
3. Arranging for the trial day.

The book also points to sources of background information and includes large repositories of both interview questions (including answers) as well as anti-patterns to look out for. Additionally, I address what equipment you should bring to your trial day, and where to get real-time help from thousands of your peers.

Prologue — Why This Book Was Written

No matter how large the pay cheque, life is just too short to spend it on unfulfilling projects!

Too often, companies advertise open positions for scrum masters or agile coaches in a way that does not reflect the state of the adoption of agile principles in their organization correctly. This often unintended mishap — a lot of companies just do not know better — can lead to mismatches which, sooner or later, will likely cause disappointments on all sides—employer, scrum master, and scrum team.

Read More: "Lipstick Agile — 13 Signs You Probably Need a New Job" and "22 Scrum Master Anti-Patterns from Job Ads."

'How to Get Hired as a Scrum Master' helps to avoid this outcome by providing a hands-on guide that allows scrum masters and agile coaches to figure out — in advance or during the application process — whether an organization is a suitable employer or client.

About the Author Stefan Wolpers

Stefan has worked many years as a product manager, product owner, and agile coach (Scrum, LeSS, Lean Startup, Lean Change). He's founded multiple companies and has led the development of B2C and B2B software, primarily for startups, but also for other organizations — including a former Google subsidiary. He is a steward of the XSCALE Alliance and an XBA Exponential Business Agility Coach (XBAC).

Stefan curates 'Food for agile Thought' — the largest weekly newsletter on agile product development with more than 13,000 subscribers. He also hosts the largest global Slack community for agile people — 'Hands-on Agile' — with more than 2,200 members. (As of January 2018.)

ABOUT THE AUTHOR STEFAN WOLPERS

Despite initially studying chemistry Stefan has never worked in a laboratory, and instead continued his education in business administration and law. Following school, he discovered a passion for software and, in 1996, launched the first online e-commerce platform to feature SAP R/3 connectivity — only to learn that the early bird does not necessarily catch the worm. After moving from his hometown of Hamburg to Berlin, Germany, Stefan created Susuh GmbH, a marketplace for local services. Other ventures followed, and in 2011 he founded Startup Camp Berlin — one of the largest German startup conferences today.

Stefan's latest project, Age of Product, focuses on the exchange of knowledge between the people involved in product development: product managers, product owners, scrum masters, designers, and developers. The goal is to help those dedicated to product development with lessons learned and best practices for continuous agile product discovery and delivery.

Read more about Stefan at LeSS Works or Scrum Alliance, and connect with him via LinkedIn, or Twitter.

PART I

THE JOB MARKET FOR SCRUM MASTERS AND AGILE COACHES

The Job Market Is Red Hot

This recent study—"LinkedIn Data Reveals the Most Promising Jobs of 2017"—listed 'scrum master' to be one of the most promising jobs of 2017:

- *Median Base Salary: $100,000*
- *Job Openings (YoY Growth): 400+ (104%)*
- *Career Advancement Score (out of 10): 8.0*
- **Top Skills:** *Agile Methodologies, Software Project Management, Scrum, Requirements Analysis, SQL*

Noting that SQL is listed as a skill prerequisite, I am not sure whether the author understands the required skill set completely. That aside, the reported rise in the number of available positions year on year (104 percent) reflects the exponential growth in the demand for scrum masters and agile coaches. (Read more on the range of scrum master salaries in the next chapter covering "The Scrum Master Salary Report 2017.")

The reasons for this are apparent — with software eating the world, and the pace of innovation accelerating as the market-entry barrier of the technology sector is continuously lowered. Venture capital is also widely available, and startups are gaining more of an innovative advantage over established organizations. Current tech trends are threatening the very existence of a lot of legacy organizations.

Read More: "Deloitte's Tech Trends 2017 Report."

Turning this legacy ship around and taking on this wave of innovative competition bow-first is a difficult thing to do for an organization founded in the golden age of Taylorism. ['Principles of Scientific Management' propounded by F.W. Taylor in 1911.] With Taylorism's structure of functional silos and command and control management style, transforming the legacy ship into a learning organization takes time. It will take because of the organizational debt, acquired over decades, results in latency that justifies using the ship/tanker metaphor in this case.

The long-established practice of legacy organizations countering this effect was to outsource innovation by acquiring promising startups. The problem with this is that the valuation of such startups has skyrocketed in recent years, while the financial prowess of legacy organizations has diminished (in many cases) at the same time. The decade-long window of opportunity in outsourcing innovation is closing.

Apart from striking the colors and admitting defeat, the only alternative is to change the legacy organization itself by transforming it into a learning organization. However, with the ensuing difficulty of refocusing everyone on creating hypotheses, running experiments, and embracing failure (while abandoning the command and control management style at the same time), legacy organizations have tended to give autonomy, accountability, and transparency a try at team level

— mostly within the product delivery organization in charge of creating software.

The rise of agile practices such as scrum can quite likely be attributed to the fact that the large consultancies (formerly die-hard proponents of Taylorism and command and control structures) are now offering professional services based on agile practices. (**For example:** "McKinsey's Digital Labs.")

Ultimately, whatever the motivation, most organizations acknowledge by now that the old way of innovating products is no longer viable — at least not in the software sector. With the desire to be agile or at least develop software in an agile way, we now observe the massive demand for scrum masters and agile coaches — with most of this demand fueled by recent converts. (In "Crossing the Chasm" terms, Agile has become mainstream as the late majority is starting to adopt Agile. (**Read More**: Moore, Geoffrey A: "Crossing the Chasm.")

Therefore, looking for a new job or client, we scrum masters and agile coaches need to answer two questions of ourselves:

- Do I want to work for a nascent agile organization (of the late majority) where my work will likely be met with resistance at multiple levels?
- If I don't want to work for a nascent agile organization, how do I identify an organization with established agile practices that are compatible with my mindset?

The two questions are relevant for both applying to available positions and identifying suitable employer or clients for a proactive application.

The Scrum Master Salary Report 2017

Now and then, the position of the scrum master is revealed as one of the top paying jobs in the United States. However, few have ventured to investigate the state of this career path on a global scale. 'The Scrum Master Salary Report 2017' is the first salary survey of its kind.

Download the free 'Scrum Master Salary Report 2017' and learn more about one of the tech industry's best career choices.

THE MAKING OF THE SCRUM MASTER SALARY REPORT 2017

We—the team of Age of Product—endeavored to unravel the career and financial background of this lucrative profession by polling scrum masters throughout the globe in the spring of 2017. Our 33 poll questions were repeatedly communicated over the course of three months during the sprint of 2017 via the Internet to thousands of scrum masters and agile coaches around the world. We utilized for this purpose Age of Product's newsletter subscriber base, the top ten LinkedIn groups on agile topics, as well as Twitter, and other channels like Medium.

The poll covered the educational background, working experience, industries, and organizational details of the companies the respondents are working for as scrum masters or agile coaches. The poll's objective was to identify common career patterns of successful scrum masters/agile coaches and link those to their financial remuneration, to provide aspiring scrum masters with an idea how to plan a future career in this promising profession.

By May 1st, 2017, an overwhelming response of over 523 individuals, from Australia to the United States, led to this final report, now available for free—the Scrum Master Salary Report 2017.

We note that data was polled via a survey sent out only in English for three months, and this may have created some bias. Regardless, we interpret and make assumptions based on the best data available. For instance, in Ireland, we had only six responses and therefore cannot easily guarantee the strength of the data. Nonetheless, based on the data received we assume here that the higher the response, the more accurate the result.

FIVE LEARNINGS FROM THE SCRUM MASTER SALARY REPORT 2017:

Analyzing the results of the poll, we discovered five exciting findings:

1. Women have astounding opportunities and salary possibilities in this field.
2. The United States is the highest paying country for scrum masters, while India is the lowest.
3. Without some form of certification, getting onto the career path is almost impossible.
4. Additional education does not affect salary.
5. Some form of previous experience is often a prerequisite.

Among the most astonishing findings in the background of scrum masters was that the wage gap between men and women is almost non-existent. The percentage of women in the role, albeit at a meager 30%, is on par with women in leadership roles (in the United States).

Additionally, it is noticeable that most of our respondents are quite optimistic about the ongoing agile transformation at their organization. Nearly 70% of our respondents have participated in agile transition before, and they are quite confident that their current transition is going in the right direction. One aspect that may play a part in this optimism is the fact that around 50% of respondents have previously worked on more than ten projects. Scrum masters already have a great deal of experience, which may translate into more trust from management and teammates.

Lastly, we now also can answer the questions whether amassing agile certifications a valuable investment from a career perspective. But see for yourself by downloading your copy of the Scrum Master Salary Report 2017.

PART II

RESEARCH: HOW TO GET AN IDEA OF AN ORGANIZATION'S AGILE MATURITY

It is impossible to assess the agile maturity of an organization solely from the outside.

However, it is possible to acquire enough of an understanding of the organization's agile practices that would foster asking the right questions at a later stage, for example during an initial job interview. Or, it may be concluded early in the assessment process (see below) that the organization is not compatible with the personal expectations of an employer or client — which is acceptable by saving wasted time and effort for all involved. Consider the popular saying: There is no project interesting enough that you just couldn't walk away from it.

The good news is that all organizations that truly embrace agile practices are usually openly talking about their journeys (unless they need to honor compliance rules), and are transparent and actively supporting the agile community. The reason for this support is simple: Being transparent and supportive is the best way to pitch the organization (and its agile culture) to prospective new team members —and the war for talent now is even more imminent for agile practitioners.

The necessity of critical information is the basis for all research activity during the three distinct phases of the assessment process, namely:

- Proactive research.
- Job advertisement, and
- Job interview.

Proactive Research

Source 1: An Opportunistic Search via Google

As a first step, always search the organization's name in combination with a variety of agile-related keywords like:

- Agile,
- Lean,
- Scrum,
- Scrum Master,
- ScrumMaster,
- Product Owner,
- Kanban,
- XSCALE,
- SAFE,
- LeSS,
- DAD,
- DevOps,
- Continuous integration,

- Continuous delivery,
- Design thinking, and
- Lean Startup.

The purpose of this exercise is to discover an organization's use of agile practices and the associated maturity level, by answering these questions:

- What are they currently practicing (Scrum, Kanban, XP, Lean UX, or Design Thinking)?
- Are the current Scrum Masters or agile coaches working at the organization?
- How many engineers or engineering teams are working for the organization?
- What is the size ratio between the product management and engineering teams?
- Is the organization practicing continuous product discovery?
- Is the organization practicing DevOps?

The initial search results will provide the first impression, directing further searches of blog posts, videos of conferences or local meetups, slide decks, podcasts, or threads in communities. A genuinely agile organization will leave traces of a large variety of content.

The mere quantity of results, though, does not signal that the organization in question has already passed the test. There is no way to avoid checking the content. Here's an example:

InfoQ — a community news site for the spread of software innovation and knowledge—has a rigorous editorial process and focuses on delivering quality content to its audience. Contrary to InfoQ's standards there are quite a few articles on Scrum Alliance, for example, that could raise eyebrows for scrutiny. These articles are often celebrating one form or another of cargo cult practices within an organization which could be masquerading as agile but is probably not agile.

A good rule of thumb when scanning search results is noting the diversity of sources. If you find content only on the company blog, and it has barely been shared or commented upon, it might hint that the content manager is either not understanding the job or the content is not relevant enough to be of interest within the agile community.

Advanced Tips: Use BuzzSumo to analyze a specific article or keyword for its popularity in social share counts. Also, search for the title of the content piece on Twitter and have a look at the search results: who from the agile community is sharing this content?

Source 2: Ask Peers for Help via Reddit, Hacker News, Slack & LinkedIn

It is also beneficial to extend the initial search to online communities such as Reddit or Hacker News (HN), to name a couple, and both communities allow for posting articles as well as questions.

The archive of HN is of particular interest — not just because of the sheer number of available articles or threads there, but also the partly heated discussions going on in the comments. Be aware, though, that 'agile' as a concept is challenged by a lot of the outspoken community members (namely, independent developers) both on Reddit and HN.

Beyond passively scanning the archives, posting a direct question to peers is an alternative. HN is likely a waste of time, and if using Reddit – choose the Subreddits /agile and /scrum for a possibly better outcome.

Note: Don't forget – haters will hate, and trolls just want to play. Do not take it personally if your search on Reddit or HN is not taking the direction you desired.

You can probably expect more support by asking the members of the "Hands-on Agile" Slack community for help. It is a worldwide community of Scrum Masters, agile coaches, and Product Owners that has proven to be very supportive. (You can sign-up for the Hands-on Agile Slack community for free.)

There are also LinkedIn groups available which focus on agile practices — some with more than 100,000 members. (For example, Scrum Alliance has a group on LinkedIn that seems more active than its online community.) After having joined them, post your question(s), remembering to be compliant with the group rules. Expect, though, your first posts to be moderated.

Some recommended LinkedIn groups are:

- Agile and Lean Software Development
- Scrum Practitioners

- Agile
- Scrum Alliance, Inc.
- Agile Project Management
- Agile Networking Group
- Lean Agile Software Development Community
- Scrum.org
- Scrum Practitioners, Scrum Masters

If posting a question to a LinkedIn group, expect to monitor it carefully and interact with answering members promptly; not communicating with responding group members may be considered rude and possibly lead to being banned from posting in the group again.

Read More: Etiquette in technology.

Lastly, try Quora — directing a question to Quora members active in the agile realm as to whether the organization of interest has an agile mindset.

Note: In doing so, avoid asking anonymous questions which tend to have a significantly lower answering rate.

Source 3: Is the Organization Sponsoring or Organizing Meetups, Barcamps, or Conferences?

Supporting public events is the highest form of contribution to the agile community by an organization. There are four different levels of engagement:

1. Organizing conferences (or Barcamps),
2. Sponsoring conferences in cash,
3. Providing speakers to conferences, and
4. Sponsoring local Meetups and Barcamps by providing a venue. (With crisps and beer!)

If an organization offers this level of support to the agile community, the talk about this will undoubtedly be on the company blog, the engineering blog, or in a press release in their public relations section.

In the unlikely case that any reference cannot be found, just contact the Public Relations department who will provide the required information.

Browsing Conference Sites for Sponsors

Conference sites are a good ground for identifying prospective organizations when considering to apply for a Scrum Master position proactively. Check carefully for two things: sponsors and speakers.

Search for sponsors that are practicing agile in their daily operations. Usually, a more significant sponsor package will include a speaking slot at the conference.

Attending such a session will provide direct access to the speaker and thus a first contact in the inner circle of that organization's agile practitioners. This access tends to be valuable: HR departments often rely on the private networks of the organization's available agile practitioners to identify suitable candidates for job openings as Scrum Master or Agile

Coach. (Accordingly, attending local Meetups can also be a worthwhile investment for job seekers.)

Note: A consultancy offers agile coaching and training jobs, so unless that type of employment is desired it might be desirable to ignore sessions provided by companies like agile42. These are the usual suspects looking for new clients or consultants among the attendees.

Browsing Conference Sites for Speakers

Personally, a more promising approach, by comparison, is to search for non-professional speakers who are aligned with an organization that is not sponsoring the conference. These speakers may indicate a suitable, prospective employer or client after already having gone through the selection process for speaking proposals and vetting of their contribution for originality.

The same approach can apply to contributions at Barcamps, although a disadvantage is that the critical information is only available during an event. While the speaker list of a conference is available in advance to stimulate ticket sales, it is the nature of a Barcamp that the schedule, and hence the speaker list, is available only on the day of the Barcamp. If already planning to attend a Barcamp, it may just be an inconvenience and not a concern. Timing is crucial, though, so please keep in mind that tickets for Barcamps are often sold out within minutes. (For example, the 400+ tickets for the UX Camp Berlin 2016 were gone in less than two minutes.)

There are numerous conferences regarding agile practices, so here are just some of them:

- Scrum Alliance Gatherings
- Agile 2018
- Agile Testing Days
- Agile on the Beach
- QCon New York
- Business Agility Conference
- Lean Kanban
- Agilia
- LeSS Conferences

For more comprehensive listings of conferences, visit:

- **Lanyrd:** Agile conferences
- **Scrum Expert:** 2018 Agile and Scrum Conferences

Lastly, the big conferences are often considered must-attend events — useful to earn Scrum Alliance SEUs or improve professional visibility within the agile industry. Alternatively, smaller conferences often prove to be more effective by providing information that helps identify a suitable, prospective agile organization. The larger the conference, the more possibility of noise camouflaging that information.

PROACTIVE RESEARCH   21

Browsing Meetup.com for Organizers

Meetup.com is a great site to discover which events of the agile community are happening locally and who is organizing them. There are thousands of Meetups around the world, covering the topics of agile frameworks and practices, software engineering, and product development in general.

Metaphorically, the low-hanging fruit is, of course, an organization that leaves a footprint in the agile community by organizing events. An excellent example of this category is Berlin-based company Zalando. Back in 2015, Zalando [Europe's largest online fashion retailer.] introduced its version of Agile, dubbed "radical agility." It has since proven to be a smashing success, not just fueling the bottom line of the business, but also the company's ambition to build an outstanding product delivery organization. A quote from its Senior Manager of Corporate Communications, Matteo Bovio:

> "Over the last year and a half, we have doubled the technology team from around 800 in 2015 to over 1,600 currently. In addition to changing our business model, we also implemented a unique culture within the technology team called Radical Agility: This has seen monthly technology applications grow from 500 to over 2,000, and allows us to ensure that we are hiring only the best quality."

Zalando is hosting several events relating to best engineering practices, as well as (generally radical) agility-related events, every month on their campus. If you want to work in an agile manner in Berlin, Zalando is certainly an organization worth considering.

Read More: "Radical Agility: How Zalando Tech Became Berlin's Hottest Workplace."

Besides spotting the Zalandos of this world, the other benefit of analyzing a local event is identifying the independent organizers in the community. Most often, these are peers dedicated to the agile cause who are giving back to the community. Given their extended networks, they are usually highly knowledgeable regarding the agile maturity level of local organizations and may know other peers that might be supportive of a quest. Reaching out to them by attending their usually free events is, therefore, a good strategy for gathering information.

Analyzing a Job Advertisement

Why Not All Job Openings Are Advertised

Not all available positions for scrum masters and agile coaches are freely advertised on the job market. If an organization can access the personal networks of its employees (or freelancers) for recommendations, it will do so. The reason for this is simple: recommendations from trusted employees often tend to be much more successful in filling a position rather than accepting one from the outside. People do care about what they help create — and this does not only apply to building products, but also to employment.

Employees are more likely to carefully consider as to whether all aspects of a friend in the profession would make a good fit for a particular position. If the friend achieves employment status, that employee will likely feel responsible for making this new relationship work in the long run — quasi-volunteering for a role as mentor. From the organization's point of view, this is a robust social contract. Usually, this mentor behavior does not even have to be incentivized since employees enjoy working with friends in their (professional) network.

Personally, this is why it is recommended to reach out to the agile community and make personal connections. It is rightly said that business is done between people, not legal entities.

Note: Be aware that eventually there is a danger of creating a hiring bias in this way. Organizations that tend only to hire people who fit well into the existing culture may be homogenizing their workforce over time. It has been proven time and again that diverse teams are more innovative. They are less biased, have different mental models in solving challenges, and suffer less from the not-invented-here syndrome.

Where to Find Job Advertisements for a Scrum Master or Agile Coach Position

One of the primary sources is the usual generic job portal goliaths (the survivors of the last Internet bubble) for such job advertisements: Monster.com, Stepstone.com, Recruit.net, or CareerBuilder.com.

One of the other sources is a first niche site, namely Scrum Alliance's *agilecareers* site, which lists more than 1,000 job openings (mostly in the USA at the moment).

Another source of advertisements may be recruiting companies or headhunters which are country-specific, for example, Hays in the UK. Lastly, there is LinkedIn which is offering thousands of available positions at the moment.

It's important to note that what separates LinkedIn from the other sites, is that LinkedIn immediately lists your contacts who work for the organization that is offering the position. If the job is of interest, you may ask one of your contacts to forward your application via the internal channels (which might be beneficial — see above section).

Analyzing a Job Advertisement for a Scrum Master or Agile Coach Position

After locating a job advertisement for a scrum master or agile coach position in the desired organization (possibly in one of those listed in the previous section), the next step is to analyze the job description.

Usually, the organization's HR department will create the final text of the job advertisement and post it to the chosen job sites. Hopefully, and depending on their process and level of collaboration (and agile mindset) in the organization, the team for which the new position was advertised may have participated in creating the advert. This indeed avoids advertising a wrong description to prospective candidates.

Too often, however, advertisements may read like a copy and paste from positions that an organization's HR believes to be similar to that of a scrum master (for example, a project manager). Or, sometimes, the HR copies from other scrum master advertisements which they believe correctly reflect the requirements of the organization. So don't be too surprised to see a job advertisement that reads like a list of scrum master anti-patterns.

This is often the case when an organization's HR does not have a lot of experience in hiring agile practitioners because they are in the early stages of the agile transition. Therefore, an unusual job description does not imply that the organization is not trying to become agile, it may just mean that the HR department has not yet caught up with the new requirements. Such an advertisement can help raise the topic and be of benefit during the job interview.

Be aware, however, that if an organization which claims to be agile is using this kind of advertisement despite being well underway on its agile transition, it then raises a red flag: miscommunication in the hiring process may indicate deeper issues or problems at the organizational level. It could be as critical as someone at management level, to whom the new scrum master would likely report, having no clue what becoming agile is all about.

As mentioned previously, here are some examples of scrum master advertisement anti-patterns (from actual job descriptions) that should raise a red flag:

- The position is labeled as
    - "Project manager/Scrum master,"
    - "Agile Project Manager," or
    - "Agile Scrum Master."
- The scrum master organizes the Scrum team's work instead of the project manager.
- The scrum master is also supposed to act as a (technical) Product Owner.
- The scrum master reports to stakeholders the output of the Scrum team (velocity, burn-down charts).

- The scrum master is supposed to handle more than one or two teams simultaneously.
- The scrum master is supposed to do secretarial work (room bookings, facilitation of ceremonies, ordering office supplies).
- The scrum master is removing impediments on behalf of the team (rather than the Scrum team becoming self-organizing).
- The scrum master is responsible for team management.
- The scrum master is responsible for the "overall delivery of the committed sprint" (whatever that refers to…).
- CSM or equivalent certification is listed as mandatory (which is a save-my-butt approach to hiring).
- The scrum master is expected:
    - To accept full responsibility for the delivery process;
    - To drive functional enhancements and continuous maintenance;
    - To communicate the company priorities and goals;
    - To maintain relevant documentation;
    - To monitor progress, risks, resources, and countermeasures in projects;
    - To prepare steering team and core team meetings;
    - To perform the Scrum Master role for "multiple flavors of agile methodologies";
    - To participate in "project plan review and provide input to ensure accuracy";
    - To "review and validate estimates for complex projects to ensure correct sizing of work";

- To provide "design thinking sessions";
- To "walk the product owner through more technical user stories."

• There is no mention of the scrum master either

- Coaching the organization, or
- Coaching the Product Owner.

My favorite anti-pattern is:

"…working reliably on projects within a given time and budget frame while maintaining our quality standards."

In other words:

"Actually, we're happy with waterfall, but the C-level wants us to be 'agile.'"

Let's close this section with an exemplary job advertisement, posted by Zalando in 2016: (Senior) Agile Coach.

Preparing for a Job Interview

Research the Interviewers

Again, the first step is to search all (known) participants of the interview. The primary interest for this is noting any content that reveals the interviewers' ideas about the 'agile mindset.' Also, note as to whether interviewers are actively doing these:

- Blogging or podcasting:
    - on the company blog,
    - on their blogs (check Medium.com directly), and
    - on industry blogs such as:
        - Dzone, https://dzone.com/
        - Agile Alliance, https://www.agilealliance.org/community/blog/
        - Scrum Alliance, https://www.scrum.org/resources/blog
        - Tech Beacon, https://techbeacon.com/
        - InfoQ, or https://www.infoq.com/

- Writing newsletters (subscribe),
- Contributing to open source software initiatives (check Github for possible repositories of interviewers),
- Twittering (what kind of content is shared), and
- Answering questions on Quora, Reddit, or Hacker News (see above).

If the organization is not sharing information on the interviewers in advance, give their HR a call and ask for it. There is no excuse for them not to provide this information in advance, so if they refuse, it should raise a red flag.

Secondly, search both Youtube and Vimeo for any videos of the interviewers, particularly those from agile conferences.

Finally, continue your research by checking the availability of the interviewers' profiles within industry organizations, for example:

- Scrum Alliance (full search function available)
- Scrum.org
- LeSS (browsing capabilities by the first letter of the last name; currently no real search function)
- SAFe (only accessible to members).

Research the Interviewers and the Organization on LinkedIn

PREPARING FOR A JOB INTERVIEW   31

Additionally, it is recommended to analyze the LinkedIn profiles of the interviewers:

- What is their job title?
- How long have they been with the organization?
- Is their current role still the first one within the organization?
- Is there a recognizable career pattern?
- What are LinkedIn groups they are members of?
- Are they actively contributing to discussions in LinkedIn groups, and if so what kind?
- Are they publishing on LinkedIn, and if so, what kind of articles?
- Are they sharing any other content?

Note: If considering an organization based in Germany, Austria, or Switzerland, consider Xing.com also for analysis.

As the last step on LinkedIn, research the organization itself — the company page as well as people working for the organization. LinkedIn offers extensive search and filter capabilities for this purpose.

Read More: "How to Use LinkedIn as a Research Engine."

Prepare the Questions to Ask During the Interview

Based on your research results, choose a list of questions to ask during the interview. Typically, five to ten questions should be more than sufficient given that interviews are timed and rarely open-ended.

A Generic Set of Questions

Previously, I created three sets of generic questions, all available from Age of Product as downloads:

1. **Cargo Cult Agile: The 'State of Agile' Checklist for Your Organization**: A list of 25 questions addressing typical anti-patterns of agile transitions
2. **20 Questions from New Scrum Master to Product Owner:** A list of 20 questions to get a new scrum master up to speed with product discovery practices
3. **20 Questions a New Scrum Master Should Ask Her Team to Get up to Speed:** A list of 20 questions a scrum master will want to ask the Scrum team when joining a new team.

All of the 65 questions in this repository are suitable to choose from for an interview. They will come in handy if there is not sufficient time to research the organization in advance.

Caution: Asking a question which can be quickly answered by searching may leave a negative impression with the interviewers: Either you did not find the time, or are not capable of answering it – which would not be favorable.

A Customized Set of Questions

Personally, a better approach is to tailor questions to the results of your research, so the interviewers notice that you did your homework. I suggest choosing the five to ten questions from either the set of generic questions (see above) or from the customized set below. These questions are the result of a canceled job podcast project. I interviewed CTOs on open positions in their product delivery organizations back in 2015, and these questions have now proven to be useful during interviews:

1. How many people are currently working for [your company]?
2. How large is the product delivery organization? (Product, UX/UI, engineering, QA, DevOps.)
3. How large is the engineering team?
4. How many engineering teams are there?
5. What technology stack are you working on?
6. What is the ratio of senior engineers to juniors engineers? (This ratio provides a good idea of the team's maturity.)
7. What tools are you using in engineering? (Github, Slack, Jira, Confluence, etc.)
8. How large is the product management team? (including those who may belong to the product organization, e.g., UX or UI designers, business analysts, et al.)
9. To whom is the product team reporting: CPO, CTO, CEO?
10. How does product discovery work at [your company]? (Or: How do you currently identify what to build?)
11. Who is building the product roadmap, if there is one? (the founders, CxO level, stakeholders and the product delivery organization including the engineers?)

12. Who is prioritizing tasks?
13. What role does the product management have in your company — ticket creator or product maker?
14. How long have you been using Scrum and how agile do you consider the organization to be? How good are you at being agile? Does the organization as well as the stakeholders understand and respect agile processes and roles? Is there a shared understanding of the product and company goals? (Or: Is the product delivery organization an isolated silo?)

    1. If so: How many team members are scrum masters or agile coaches? (Note: This number compared to the size of engineering teams is a good indicator of its level of agility.)
    2. If so: How many teams will I be required to work with as scrum master or agile coach?

15. How are multiple teams aligned? Are you using scaling frameworks like SAFe, LeSS, or DAD?
16. Does each product manager have its team? Is a product manager working with either a dedicated team or several teams, depending on the tasks? How large is your product organization and how is it organized? (Note: If the company's product delivery organization is huge, scaling agile methodologies might become a challenge within the organization.)

    1. If so: Are you working in cross-functional teams? (Note: A cross-functional team consists of engineers, UX/UI designers, QA engineers and often a dedicated product manager/product owner. A cross-functional can autonomously deliver value to customers.)
    2. If so: How many team members have a UX

PREPARING FOR A JOB INTERVIEW

background? (Note: This number compared to the size of the product delivery organization is a good indicator of agility — hence the product management team's level of autonomy.)

17. What would you consider to be your product team's level of autonomy? (Example: Delegation Poker [A management self-organization game.] levels — from "Tell": you as the manager make the decision (no autonomy), to "Delegate": you offer no influence and let the team work it out (full autonomy).

With this advice, you should have a file on the organization and the chosen interview questions available to guide you through the first interview.

The next chapter addresses interview questions likely to be asked.

PART III

THE INTERVIEW: 47 SCRUM MASTER INTERVIEW QUESTIONS

The original set of interview questions back from January 2016 — "Hiring: 38 Scrum Master Interview Questions to Avoid Agile Imposters" — was written for a hiring organization. The problem back then was, and it still is today, that a lot of candidates for a scrum master or agile coach position had neither the experience nor the skill set required to contribute in a meaningful way to a transition of an organization.

Up to January 2018, the PDF with the interview questions has been downloaded almost 11,000 times and can be considered an integral part of the hiring process of many organizations. And as I believe in empathy, I deliberately left the text unchanged. Try walking in the shoes of the hiring company for a while.

Set 1: The Role of the Scrum Master

Background

- Scrum is not a methodology, but a framework. There are no rules that apply to every scenario — just best practices that have worked before in other organizations.
- The best practices of other organizations cannot just be copied to your own. Every best practice requires a particular context to work.
- As somebody hiring an agile team, you need to determine for yourself what works for your organization — which is a process, not a destination.
- The role of a scrum master is primarily one of leadership and coaching. It is not a management role.
- A scrum master should recognize that different stages of a scrum team's [1] development require different approaches: some, teaching; some, coaching; and some, mentoring.
- A scrum master should know of the Shu-Ha-Ri (Japanese martial arts) method of learning new techniques.
- A scrum master's principal objective should be to remove

themselves from daily operations by enabling the scrum team to be self-organizing and self-managing.
- Being a scrum master does not entail, and should never entail, enforcing processes.
- Scrum is not designed for bean counters, although some metrics are helpful in understanding the health of a scrum team. Insisting that the team achieve specific KPI [2] (e.g., commitments vs. velocity) does not help.
- Scrum doesn't elaborate on the process that enables a product owner to add valuable, usable, and feasible user stories to the product backlog [3]. Product discovery using the Design Thinking, Lean Startup, or Lean UX methodologies may help, but in any case, a good scrum master will want the scrum team to be a part of this process (whether participating in user interviews or running experiments).
- A scrum team's communication with stakeholders should not be run through a gatekeeper (e.g., solely by the product owner) because this hurts transparency and negatively affects the team's performance. Sprint reviews [4], conversely, are an excellent way to stay in close contact with stakeholders and to present the value delivered by the team during each previous sprint [5].

Question 01

The Agile Manifesto infers people over processes. Isn't a scrum master — whose role is meant to enforce the process — therefore a *contradiction?*

A scrum master does not wield any real authority. The scrum team does not report to them. This question is meant to help reveal whether your candidate understands that their role is to lead — as opposed to managing — the team. Asking this question is also likely to show why your candidate is interested in the position of a scrum master in the first place.

Acceptable answers should emphasize facilitation and support:

- "I am the facilitator for the scrum team. It's my job to make them successful."
- "I am neither a project manager nor a people manager. I support the scrum team in achieving self-management. I do not tell people what to do."
- "I am the scrum team's facilitator as teacher, coach, or mentor, encouraging them to excel as an agile team."

Question 02

What indicators might there be that demonstrate agile practices are working for your organization, and which of these would prove your efforts at becoming agile are succeeding?

There is no standard or general definition of 'agile success' that can be used to measure an organization's agility. Every organization must develop its criteria. A growing team velocity [6] is usually not considered to be a meaningful indicator (see Question 40 for a discussion of team velocity).

However, although mostly indirect, there are various indicators that may be useful in determining success:

- Improved team happiness is exhibited by reduced churn and an increase in the number of referrals from members.
- Increased competitiveness in the battle for talent can be demonstrated by an increase in the number of experienced people willing to join the organization.
- Products delivered to customers are resulting in higher retention rates, better conversion rates, increased lifetime value, and similar improvements to the business.
- Increased software quality can be demonstrated by measurably less technical debt [7], fewer bugs, and less time spent on maintenance.
- Production time, from validated idea to shipped product, has been reduced.
- The cycle time [8] for hypothesis validation has been reduced.
- There has been a reduced allocation of resources to low-value products.
- There is greater respect among stakeholders for the IT team.
- Stakeholders are increasingly participating in agile meetings, especially during the sprint demo [9].

Question 03

Should a scrum master remove impediments on behalf of the scrum team?

A scrum master should not be concerned with "removing impediments on behalf of the scrum team," no matter how often this requirement is mentioned in job advertisements. If a scrum master acts like a 'scrum mom,' their team will never become self-organizing.

A scrum team must make its own decisions. This process almost inevitably results in failures, dead-ends, and other unplanned excursions when the team is learning something new. Consequently, in the beginning, a team will need more guidance than usual from the scrum master — and of a different kind than exemplified by drawing offline boards (see Questions 31 and 32) or updating tickets in JIRA [10]. Such guidance should not, however, become an exercise in protective parenting — a team must be allowed to learn from their failures.

Read more: "Scrum Master Anti Patterns: Beware of Becoming a Scrum Mom (or Scrum Pop)."

Question 04

How should a scrum master communicate with a product owner?

Communicating honestly and openly is the best way for a scrum master to get the cooperation of a product owner. Both must serve as leaders without being authoritative, and each depends upon the other working reciprocally for a scrum team's success (e.g., accomplishing a sprint's goal). They are allies concerning coaching the organization to become, and remain, agile.

A product owner is responsible for providing prompt feedback on product matters, for clarifying goals, and for ensuring that the entire product delivery team [11] understands the product vision.

A scrum master, in return, supports the product owner in building a high-value product backlog, and to this end must facilitate active collaboration between the product owner and the scrum team.

Question 05

Should the scrum team become involved in the product discovery process and, if so, how?

There are two principal reasons why a scrum team should be involved in the product discovery process as early as possible:

1. The sooner engineers participate in the product discovery process, the lesser the chances solutions will be pursued that are technically not viable or would not result in a return on investment.
2. Involving a scrum team early on ensures that the team and its product owner develop a shared understanding and ownership of what will be built. This helps significantly with allocating resources to the right issues, maximizing value for the customer, and mitigating investment risk.

Involving a scrum team's engineers early in the process ensures their buy-in, and the team's willingness to participate in all phases of a product's development. This motivates the team to participate when making changes necessary to accomplish the goals defined for each sprint or product release.

Question 06

The role of the product owner is a bottleneck by design. How do you support the product owner so that they maximize value?

This question revisits the previous. Again, your candidate should focus on explaining why involving the scrum team early in the product discovery process is beneficial for both the product owner and the organization. The team either wins together or loses together.

Question 07

How can you ensure that a scrum team has access to a project's stakeholders?

When answering this question, your candidate should explain that there is no easy way to ensure access to stakeholders.

Your candidate might suggest encouraging stakeholders to engage in practical (transparent, helpful) communication. Sprint reviews are a useful venue for this, and the interaction often promotes better relationships between different departments and business units.

Question 08

How do you promote an agile mindset across departmental boundaries and throughout an organization

and, in pursuit of that, what is your strategy when coaching stakeholders not familiar with IT?

There are various tactics a scrum master can use to engage stakeholders with scrum:

- Most importantly, a scrum master should live and breathe the principles of the Agile Manifesto. They should talk to everyone in the organization involved in building the product, and they should be transparent about what they do. (**Read more**: "10 Proven Stakeholder Communication Tactics During an Agile Transition.")
- Product and engineering teams can produce evidence, in presentations or otherwise, proving to stakeholders that scrum is significantly reducing the lead time from idea to product launch.
- Product and engineering teams can demonstrate that scrum mitigates risk (for example, the prediction of when new features could be made available), thus contributing to other departments' successes in planning and execution.
- A scrum team can be transparent concerning their work and proactively engage stakeholders by inviting them to meetings, sprint reviews, and other events where the team communicates their activity or progress.
- Training for everyone in the organization, particularly the stakeholders, is essential. One hands-on approach is to organize workshops designed to teach agile techniques for non-technical colleagues.

Question 09

How would you introduce scrum to senior executives?

This is a deliberately open question meant to encourage discussion. In answering this question, your candidate should elaborate on how they would spread an agile mindset throughout an organization or, ideally, and more specifically, how they would create a learning organization that embraces experimentation to identify the best product for its customers.

A good candidate is likely to talk about the necessity of 'selling' agile to the organization to win the hearts and minds of the stakeholders. At the beginning of a transition any organization shows inertia to change, so to overcome this resistance executives and stakeholders need to know how agile will benefit them before they're likely to commit.

Read more: "The Big Picture of Agile: How to Pitch the Agile Mindset to Stakeholders."

One practical approach when introducing scrum to senior executives is to organize workshops for C-level management. Applying scrum at the executive level has been successful in the past. Executives, and potentially even directors, can gain a first-hand experience with agile methodologies if organized as a scrum team.

There are no right or wrong answers to this question. Best practices need to take into consideration an organization's culture, size, product maturity, legal and compliance requirements, and the industry it's operating in.

Question 10

You've already provided your project's stakeholders with

training in scrum. After the initial phase of trying to apply the concepts, when the very first obstacles are encountered, some of these stakeholders begin to resist continued adoption. What is your strategy for and experience in handling these situations?

This question is meant to encourage an exchange of ideas about, and lessons learned when overcoming resistance to agile within an organization. Familiarity with agile failure patterns that are common to many organizations will demonstrate your candidate's experience. We have published a list of agile failure patterns at Age of Product.

Your candidate should also be familiar with the particular challenge middle managers face in any transition to agile practices. Moving from a command-and-control style (for example, managing people and telling them what to do) to a servant-leadership style — thus abandoning Taylor's principles [12] — is not for everyone.

Read more: "Why Agile Turns Into Micromanagement."

[1] The scrum team comprises less than ten members who are cross-functional and do the work necessary to create a product increment.

[2] Key Performance Indicators are metrics used to evaluate an organization's success at reaching targets.

[3] Product backlog is a list of items to work on, such as bugs, technical work, and knowledge acquisition.

[4] Sprint reviews involve discussion of both planned work not completed in a sprint and demonstration of completed work to the shareholders.

[5] A basic unit of development in scrum, the planned sprint is restricted to a specific duration of the team.

[6] Team velocity is a measurement of work completed within a given period based upon relevant comparisons.

[7] Technical debt is the extra development work that arises when code that is easier or faster to implement in the short run is used instead of applying the best overall solution.

[8] The cycle time is the number of days passed between starting and ending an experiment suitable to validate or falsify the underlying hypothesis.

[9] Part of the sprint review, the demo is when the scrum team presents the completed work to the stakeholders.

[10] A proprietary issues tracking and project management software system, JIRA® is a registered trademark of Atlassian Pty Ltd.

[11] A product delivery team comprises everyone involved in delivering a product to market, including the scrum teams involved.

[12] F.W. Taylor's principles of scientific management are an industrial era organization and management theory according to which workers are seen as commodities and should be managed as such.

Set 2: Backlog Refinement and Estimation

Background

- Estimation and backlog refinement are essential tasks for every scrum team. Although the product owner (at least officially) is in charge of keeping the product backlog at 'peak value delivery,' they need the assistance of the entire team to do so.
- A cross-functional and co-located scrum team working independently of other teams is an ideal scenario. The reality is that most scrum teams will often be dependent upon deliveries from other teams (for example, API endpoints [1]) and deliverables from the UX [2] or UI [3] department.
- There are two essential ingredients for good scrum team performance:
    - **Writing the user story [4] as a team.** When something should be built, the product owner first explains why and provides the necessary background (i.e., market intelligence, results from experiments, user interviews, statistical data). Writing user stories, then, is a corresponding and collaborative effort involving the entire

scrum team. The process should create a shared understanding of what will be built and for what reasons (the product owner providing the 'why,' the scrum team detailing the 'how,' both defining the 'what'), and a shared sense of ownership among team members.

- **Sharing a definition of ready.** To ensure a flow of well-drafted user stories for the development process, the scrum team and the product owner need to agree on a definition of ready (see Question 15) for these stories. This definition is an agreement about what needs to be provided for a user story to be considered ready for estimation. If even one of the defined requirements is not met, a user story isn't ready for estimation. A user story without a previous estimation is an unknown entity and, therefore, not ready to be made part of a sprint backlog [5] because a scrum team can't commit to an unknown entity in a sprint. Consequently, the scrum team must learn to say 'No.'

- A well-groomed product backlog probably has user stories detailed for about two or three sprints, and perhaps less than half of these stories conform to the scrum team's definition of ready. There may also be additional user stories that no one except the product owner is working on at the moment.

Question 11

The product owner for your scrum team frequently turns requirements documents received from stakeholders into tickets and asks you to estimate each. How do you feel about this procedure?

SET 2: BACKLOG REFINEMENT AND ESTIMATION 53

A product owner should never turn requirements documents [6] received from stakeholders into tickets, and a scrum master should never accept such a procedure. It's nothing more than a waterfall process [7] dressed-up in a pseudo-agile methodology.

If an organization is supposed to focus on delivering value to its customers, it is essential that any process involving 'requirements' being handed down to its engineers by a project manager be abandoned. It makes no difference if the project manager is posing as a product owner. Instead, the organization should start including everyone in the product discovery process, thereby ensuring a shared vision of what needs to be built.

Question 12

What kind of information would you require from the product owner to provide your team with an update on the product and market situation?

Information that a scrum master might require from a product owner when wanting to update their team on the product, or a market's reaction to it, would include any information that could provide the scrum team with an understanding of why something is of value to customers. Such information may be of a quantitative nature (e.g., analytical data describing how a process is utilized) or of a qualitative nature (e.g., transcripts, screencasts, or videos from a user testing session).

Excellent suggestion on the part of your candidate would

be for the scrum team to participate in gathering qualitative signals by taking part in user interviews.

Question 13

Who should be writing user stories?

Writing user stories should be a joint effort by all members of a scrum team. If it's not, the team might not feel that they have ownership of the stories — inevitably leading to less or no commitment, reduced motivation, and ultimately a lower-quality product.

Question 14

What does a good user story look like? What is its structure?

A good user story:

- Includes a description,
- Has acceptance criteria defined,
- Can be delivered within a single sprint,
- Has all UI deliverables available,
- Identifies all (probable) dependencies,
- Has performance criteria defined,
- Has tracking criteria established, and
- Is estimated by the scrum team.

Question 15

What should a definition of ready consist of?

A 'definition of ready' is an agreement between the scrum team and the product owner about what must be included in a user story (before the story can be considered ready for estimation). It defines what a good user story looks like.

The discussion in Question 14 includes an outline of what a good user story should consist of. Another approach, however, is to use a framework for user stories — such as the INVEST mnemonic by Bill Wake:

- **Independent.** The user story should be self-contained, in a way that there is no inherent dependency on another user story.
- **Negotiable.** Until becoming part of an iteration, user stories can always be changed and rewritten.
- **Valuable.** A user story must deliver value to the end user.
- **Estimable.** You must always be able to estimate the size of a user story.
- **Small.** User stories should not be so big as to become impossible to plan, task, and prioritize with some certainty.
- **Testable.** The user story (or its related description) must provide the necessary information to make test development possible.

Question 16

Why aren't user stories simply estimated in staff-hours?

Estimating user stories in staff-hours is never a good idea. It intentionally diverts the emphasis away from the real purpose of the estimation process: to create a shared understanding of the task ahead among all members of the scrum team. Ergo, the estimate itself is just a byproduct.

Estimating is often tricky when:

- Legacy software is involved,
- A team is facing significant technical debt, or
- A team is composed of mostly junior members.

Story points [8] are much better suited to estimating than staff-hours in all situations, but especially in tricky situations, because they accurately reflect both the complexity of the task and the effort required to complete it. Using man-hours instead of story points typically shifts the focus from value creation for customers to the more traditional project management of costs and budgeting, effectively imposing a waterfall process.

A good candidate would mention the ongoing discussion in the agile community as to whether estimations are useful in general. They would also likely point to the 'no estimates' (#noestimates) concept.

Question 17

The product owner of your scrum team tends to add ideas of all kinds to the product backlog as a reminder to work on them at a later stage. Over time, this has led to over 200 tickets in various stages. What are your thoughts on this? Can a scrum teamwork on 200 tickets?

SET 2: BACKLOG REFINEMENT AND ESTIMATION

Any product backlog larger than the scope of two or three sprints is not manageable. Misusing a backlog by adding hundreds of items to it is a clear sign that the product owner needs help from the scrum team or the scrum master to better cope with an influx of ideas, suggestions, and requirements. A smaller backlog avoids misallocating resources; a larger backlog is an indication of waste.

Your candidate should make it clear that they would support a product owner in dealing with the size of the product backlog, and with processing input from stakeholders.

[1] An Application Programming Interface endpoint is a URL and the commands that may be issued through it, for use within the software to instruct other software.

[2] User Experience is a process of tasks focused on the optimization of a product for improving user satisfaction.

[3] User Interface design complements the UX in the presentation and interactivity of a product.

[4] An Agile software development tool, a user story talks about the desired functionality of a requirement.

[5] The prioritized list of chosen tasks to be completed during a sprint is known as the sprint backlog.

[6] Requirements documents might include, for example, software requirements specifications (SRS).

[7] The waterfall model is the sequential design process traditionally used in software development.

[8] Story points are units of measure expressing estimates of the overall effort required to implement a product backlog item fully.

Set 3: Sprint Planning

Background

- It used to be that a product owner would explain high-value user stories in a product backlog to the scrum team during sprint planning. The team would then turn these into more detailed user stories, and estimate the subsequent stories. There is now, however, a consensus among agile practitioners that working on these high-level user stories in separate backlog refinement and estimation meetings — before sprint planning — actually improves the quality of the stories and thus the outcome of the team's work.
- Sprint planning can create a sense of ownership among a scrum team's members by enabling them to make a solid commitment to the items in the sprint backlog. But this only happens if a team's uncertainty about the quality of the user stories they're receiving is eliminated. To be sure that their team can be confident, a scrum master should run weekly product backlog refinement and estimation sessions, only allowing into sprint planning those user stories that meet the team's 'definition of ready' standard.
- Sprint planning should typically be divided into two parts:
    - **Sprint planning I**. During the first part of sprint planning,

a product owner presents to the scrum team the product owner's choice of the most valuable user stories from the product backlog as a ranked list. The team then selects from the top of the list down those stories it can commit to delivering by the end of the sprint — taking into consideration their present constraints including, for example, available capacity, or the required technical tasks that need to be addressed during the same sprint.
  - **Sprint planning II**. During the second part of sprint planning, the scrum team adds detail to the user stories in the sprint backlog (for example, splitting the stories into tasks, identifying elements of the stories that need further clarification, and agreeing on who will be working on what tasks). The product owner does not necessarily need to participate in this second part of sprint planning but does need to be available to answer questions that the team may have.
- If user story preparation is handled well, an entire sprint planning session might be completed in less than 2 or 3 hours.
- Productive sprint planning requires a healthy scrum team. Dysfunctional teams will not achieve the necessary level of cooperation. Sprint planning with dysfunctional teams will only result in a futile and painful exercise.
- A scrum team should usually avoid allocating more than 80% of their capacity to new tasks — including user stories, technical tasks, bugs, and probably spikes [1]. Flow theory [2] shows that a 90% or higher allocation of available capacity will not lead to a team achieving their peak performance.
- Bugs, refactoring, and research all require regular attention to avoid building-up technical debt. An effective scrum team allocates at least 25% of their capacity to these tasks.

- Incomplete and poorly prepared user stories severely hamper the effectiveness of a scrum team. These stories should never be selected for the sprint backlog, but instead sorted out during backlog refinement and estimation meetings.

Question 18

How can a scrum master contribute to sprint planning in a way that enables the scrum team to work only on the most valuable user stories?

It is the prerogative of the product owner to define the scope of an upcoming sprint by identifying and prioritizing the most valuable user stories in the product backlog, and the scrum master must support the product owner in this. Pursuant, the best way for a scrum master to ensure that a scrum team is working on the most valuable user stories is to ensure that:

1. The scrum team is involved in the product discovery process at an early stage;
2. The product backlog refinement process is well understood by both the scrum team and the product owner (this should be supported, for example, by the creation of a 'definition of ready' standard for user stories); and
3. All user stories are created in a collaborative effort between the product owner and the scrum team (the goal being a shared understanding of the user stories and thus joint ownership).

Your candidate should note that although the product owner defines the scope of the sprint (and the sprint's goal), it is the prerogative of the scrum team to address technical debt and bugs during the same sprint (a team should be able to allocate up to 25% of their available capacity for this).

Question 19

With what metrics would you assess the value of a user story?

There are quantitative as well as qualitative measurements that may be used to assess the value of a user story or whether the investment is worthwhile. These may include

- revenue increases,
- cost cutting benefits achieved by internal process improvements,
- increases in customer satisfaction rates (NPS [3]),
- increases in signups for new products, or
- positive customer feedback received from the customer care team.

Question 20

How do you facilitate user story selection in a way that the most valuable stories are chosen without overruling the scrum team's prerogative to define their commitment?

If a scrum team is involved early enough in either user story selection (preferably by jointly creating the stories with the product owner) or product discovery, a scrum master will probably not need to guide the team that the most valuable stories are chosen. Most teams will support the product owner's choice of user stories for a given sprint.

If a team resorts to cherry picking — choosing user stories only to satisfy personal preferences — during sprint planning, the backlog refinement process needs to be seriously inspected. In all likelihood, the product owner is choosing user stories that are not maximizing customer value.

Question 21

How much of a scrum team's capacity during a regular sprint would you consider adequate for refactoring: fixing important bugs or exploring new technologies or ideas?

Apart from sprints during which there are critical and urgent tasks to address (such as fixing a problem that has taken the website offline), a good rule of thumb is a 15-10-5 allocation of a scrum team's capacity to refactoring, bug fixing, and research. Specifically, this means dedicating:

- 15% of a team's capacity for technical debt,
- 10% of a team's capacity for bugs, and
- 5% of a team's capacity to explorative spikes (when potentially helpful).

A scrum team may, of course, deviate from this when it comes to individual sprints. But, generally, consistently making these allocations will satisfy both the code quality and maintenance requirements of most software applications.

Question 22

Should a product owner assign user stories or tasks to individual members of a scrum team?

A product owner individually assigning user stories to members of a scrum team is not agile, and if a product owner is doing this, they need to be stopped. Scrum teams are supposed to be self-organizing. The assignment of user stories and the distribution of tasks among the members of a scrum team is the prerogative of the team itself. Preventing this error should be one of the scrum master's most pressing concerns.

Question 23

How do you deal with team members cherry-picking tasks?

A scrum team has autonomy in how its members choose to distribute tasks, so it may be that the presumed cherry-picking of tasks is, in fact, a valuable and crucial part of the team's path to performance. However, if team members are complaining about how the others are choosing their tasks, the scrum master needs to address the issue. Additional training might help some team members accommodate a greater variety of tasks. Or, perhaps, other team members may need to be gently pushed out of their comfort zone so that they will more readily choose different kinds of tasks over what they've become accustomed to.

Question 24

A user story is lacking the final user interface designs, but the design team promises to deliver on day two of the upcoming sprint. The product owner for your team is okay with that and pushes to have the user story added to the sprint backlog. What are your thoughts on this scenario?

Whether an incomplete user story should be added to the sprint backlog depends upon the team's present concerns and experience with the circumstances that caused the story not to meet their definition of ready. In the case of an incomplete or missing user interface (UI) design, for example, if the design team is almost sure to deliver because they have done so in the past, and if the user story is high value, and if the story can be accomplished within the sprint despite its UI deliverables arriving late, and if the team agrees to it — then an exception may be acceptable.

Beware that exceptions tend to become accepted practices. An organization intent on being agile should not be allowed to bypass the backlog refinement and sprint planning process. Your candidate should be aware that such situations are not tenable. Furthermore, if the implementation of a user story subjected to such an exception fails, no one will bother to read the fine print and acknowledge that an exception had been made. Instead, they will most likely view the agile process itself as having failed.

Your candidates may either accept or reject exceptions to the agile process. But they should also be able to analyze situations in which exceptions have been made, and explain the collateral damage that the scrum team may be exposed to.

Question 25

A member of the scrum team does not want to participate in sprint planning and considers the meetings a waste of time. How do you deal with this attitude?

If the member of a scrum team does not want to participate in sprint planning and considers the meetings a waste of time, they're exhibiting a type of passive-aggressive behavior. Although not particular to scrum, this is a problem because the underlying attitude is toxic and will affect both team-building and team performance.

When the member of a scrum team behaves as described, the team's scrum master needs to take action. Counterproductive behavior can neither be ignored nor tolerated if the team is to continue functioning. Effective action is likely to require a series of escalating steps:

1. The scrum master should start by addressing the team member privately to discuss their reservations and, perhaps, more coaching or a longer training period.
2. Following private discussion, the entire team can be involved by making the team member's reservations a topic of discussion during one or more retrospectives (see Set 5). This enables the team to offer their support.
3. If there is still no change in the team member's attitude, a meeting with the team member and their manager is advisable.
4. If no change can be achieved, it might be possible to reassign the team member to another (probably non-agile) team, or to a kanban team unlikely to force the team member out of their comfort zone.

Situations such as described highlight how scrum is not meant for everybody.

[1] A spike is a small task done to reduce uncertainty about a larger task.

[2] Flow theory is an optimal psychological state experienced, resulting in immersion and concentrated focus on a task.

[3] Net Promoter Score ® is a customer loyalty metric and registered trademark of Fred Reichheld, Bain & Company, and Satmetrix Systems.

Set 4: Standups

Background

- Standups are meetings well suited to discuss a current sprint's progress: is all going as planned, or does the scrum team need to adjust?
- Standups are a convenient time for a scrum team to meet and communicate with a project's stakeholders.
- Standups cannot fix, among other things: a dysfunctional organization, a dysfunctional scrum team, an inadequate product backlog, a sprint planning session gone wrong, low-quality user stories, or a missing product vision.
- Standups are valuable if the scrum team is already collaborating well and the basics — such as the product backlog, and sprint planning — are in order.
- The more experienced a scrum team, and the better the internal communications, the more a standup will seem a time-consuming ritual of little value.
- An advanced scrum team may consider virtual meetings instead of real meetings using, for example, a Slack [1] channel.
- A two-person scrum team does not necessarily need a

formal standup — meeting for coffee would be a practical alternative.

- There is something wrong with a scrum team who do not communicate impediments to their scrum master before each standup. It's possible they're acting more like a group of friends than a scrum team.
- Standups are not reporting sessions for the benefit of product owners or participating stakeholders.
- Offline boards are valuable: physically taking a card and moving it instills a certain ownership of a user story. If you have to let go of either an online or offline board and you're a co-located team, consider letting go of the online board.

Question 26

Would you recommend formal standups for all teams, no matter the size or experience level?

In answering this question, your candidate should exhibit common sense regarding formal standups. Standups are an essential part of scrum, but not all standups need to be formal. A small, experienced, and co-located team may use a coffee break for their standup.

However, taking that kind of relaxed approach to standups for a large team with several junior members would probably achieve nothing — if it doesn't first descend into chaos. For large teams, a formal meeting is needed to provide format and guidance.

For distributed teams who can't quickly meet for coffee, a formal standup is necessary to accommodate technical constraints and must be scheduled and conducted in an organized fashion.

Question 27

Do you expect experienced team members to wait until the next standup to ask for help overcoming an impediment?

When impeded, members of a scrum team should never need to wait, neither for a standup nor any other event, to ask for help. A team waiting to ask for help is a team delaying progress. If the more experienced members of a scrum team are waiting for the next standup before either asking for help or themselves dealing with an impediment, the scrum master has team-building work to do.

Question 28

How do you handle team members who 'lead' standups, turning the event into a reporting session for themselves?

There are no official leadership roles in scrum. However, it's not uncommon for some members of a scrum team to assume leadership. This typically happens when a particular team member possesses superior (technical) expertise, communication skills, or just a higher level of engagement.

All teams go through Tuckman's stages of group development: forming, norming, storming, and performing. Scrum teams are no exception.

It's important that when a member of a scrum team assumes leadership, this does not result in other members reporting to them. A scrum master must be vigilant and intervene if necessary to ensure that all team members communicate and work together — during standups and otherwise — in the spirit of scrum.

Question 29

How do you manage team members who consider standups to be a waste of time and are therefore either late, uncooperative, or simply don't attend?

Refer to Question 25, where addressing this similar attitude or behavioral problem is discussed at length. Your candidate's answers should address those same points.

Question 30

Your team's standups are not attended by any stakeholder. How do you change that?

Asking this question can easily spark a philosophical discussion about whether stakeholders should be allowed to participate in a scrum team's standups (also known as the 'daily scrums'). Try to avoid this.

If stakeholders participate in a team's standups, is it likely to result in the form of reporting that circumvents scrum rules? Not necessarily. It's good if some adaptation of scrum can be made to work for an organization. Allowing stakeholders to participate in standups need not be ruled out if the team finds it acceptable. In fact, if stakeholders attend standups regularly, this invariably and significantly improves communication between a team and their stakeholders.

So how does a scrum master encourage stakeholders to attend standups? By making it worth their while. The scrum master might achieve this in any number of ways: for example, they might offer stakeholders the opportunity to learn early details of a new product or feature, or they might choose to give stakeholders the opportunity to ask questions of the engineers directly (without otherwise going through the product owner).

Question 31

How do you approach standups with distributed teams?

Standups for scrum teams whose members are distributed between different offices or working remotely are not much different to standups for scrum teams whose members are co-located. The exception is that distributed teams sharing board activity may require video conferencing when working with offline boards that mirror each other.

If a scrum team is using online task management or planning software like JIRA [2], the team's boards can be online, and updates can take place on-screen. This makes it easy for members of a distributed team to follow board activity. With online boards in place, a Skype or Google Hangouts [3] call will likely be enough for a distributed team to have their standup.

Question 32

Can you draw an example of a scrum team's offline kanban board — right now?

In this question, the qualifier 'Kanban' is used as a teaser. Anyone interviewing for the role of scrum master should be able to draw a simple offline board.

The columns (or rows) of an offline board should usually include (in consecutive order)

1. Backlog
2. In progress
3. Code review
4. Quality assurance
5. Done

Additional information may be included on or attached to any board:

- Sprint or meeting dates
- User acceptance tests (UAT)
- A definition of ready
- A burndown chart (progress and work remaining over time)
- A parking lot (topics for future discussion)

Your candidate should mention that a scrum master is not obliged to provide the scrum team with an offline board. A board is the responsibility of the team working with it. The scrum master should, however, provide an introductory workshop on the subject if no member of the team is familiar with offline boards.

Read more: "How to Build Offline Boards."

[1] Slack is a popular online messaging software for team communication and collaboration.

[2] JIRA ® is a proprietary issue tracking and project management software, and a registered trademark of Atlassian Pty Ltd.

[3] Skype and Google Hangouts are popular computer-based telephony applications.

Set 5: Retrospectives

Background

- Retrospectives should encourage self-expression, thereby making it easier for a scrum team to uncover the concerns and frustrations that its members may be harboring so that strategies may be devised to overcome them.
- Retrospectives will only improve a team's collaboration and performance if the team considers these meetings a safe place to provide honest and constructive feedback.
- The blame game is not helpful. During a retrospective, the members of a scrum team should focus on how to improve a situation — and avoid blaming one another.
- Some scrum teams always include the product owner in their retrospectives, while other teams insist that the product owner should be expressly invited.
- It's best not to hold retrospectives at a team's workplace. Distance makes it easier for team members to reflect on the sprint. It's also helpful to regularly change locations for the meeting. Being in a new locale helps to prevent boredom (and team members 'checking out' altogether).
- The format for a scrum team's retrospectives should

regularly be changed. The same format should not be run more than twice.

- Smartphones, tablets, and laptops should not be permitted at retrospectives so that the members of the scrum team are not distracted, and can focus on contributing to the meeting.

- All issues, concerns, and frustrations, should be documented — even if just temporarily using sticky notes. Though it's always better to keep a formal document or file.

- Retrospectives must produce answers to specific questions. The **'classic'** set of questions includes:

  - What went right?
  - What went wrong?
  - What is there to improve?

- An alternative set of questions is the **'starfish'** retrospective:

  - What to introduce?
  - What to keep doing?
  - What to stop doing?
  - What to do more of?
  - What to do less of?

- An alternative to asking questions at a retrospective is to employ the Glad, Sad, Mad [1] technique. This technique works best following either:

  - a long interval (For example, at the end of the year),
  - a major change,
  - a major drawback,
  - unusual pressure, or

SET 5: RETROSPECTIVES

- ○ an outstanding achievement made by the team.
- According to Diana Larsen and Esther Derby in their book Agile Retrospectives: Making Good Teams Great, there are five stages to running a retrospective: setting the stage, gathering data, generating insights, deciding what to do, and closing the retrospective.
- A retrospective should set SMART [2] goals for action items (the tasks to be done):
  - ○ Action items should be specific and measurable ("do X more often" does not meet that criteria).
  - ○ A single member of the scrum team should be made responsible for each action item.
  - ○ Each action item should include an estimate of when results can be expected.
  - ○ Action items should be placed on a whiteboard to make tracking progress visual and more prominent.
- Every new retrospective should start with reviewing the status of the action items decided upon during the previous retrospective.

Question 33

Who should participate in a retrospective?

Only the immediate members of a scrum team should participate in that team's retrospectives. Especially important is that the managers of a team's members not be present.

The only exception is the product owner. It's a good idea

to include the product owner in a scrum team's retrospectives because the product owner is a crucial member of the larger team. But it's not mandatory. Some teams may prefer that the product owner not participate — and a team's wishes must always be considered.

Question 34

Should you check a team's health during a retrospective, or is doing so unnecessary? If you do, how would you go about it?

Measuring the health of a scrum team — that is, getting an idea about current levels of engagement and satisfaction — is useful for identifying trends that may affect productivity.

One effective method of measuring the health of a scrum team is to circulate a multiple choice questionnaire at the team's retrospectives. A survey that requires just two minutes to complete and uses a simple scale for each of the questions — from 1 (terrible) through 2 (poor), 3 (neutral), 4 (good), to 5 (excellent) — is usually best. During the retrospective, upon completing the questionnaire, the team should discuss the results with an aim to uncover any concerns or frustrations they may be harboring.

Question 35

What retrospective formats have you used in the past?

There are various retrospective formats in use, and each is meant to accommodate different situations. Your candidate should have experience applying more than one of these formats, and should be able to share their logic for having done so:

The classic format:

- What did we do well?
- What should we have done better?

The boat format:

- What's pushing us forward?
- What's holding us back?

The starfish retrospective:

- Start doing
- Do less of
- Do more of
- Stop doing
- Continue doing

The Diana Larsen and Esther Derby format [3]:

- Set the stage
- Gather data
- Generate insights
- Decide what to do
- Close the retrospective.

Question 36

How do you prevent boredom during retrospectives?

When required to attend a boring retrospective, members of a scrum team will become bored.

There are many possibilities for variation that can be used to prevent a retrospective from being boring, and team members from becoming bored. A different location, a different format, and shortening or lengthening the allotted time box are just some of the variations that can be tried. Scrum masters might also use a team's choice of action items to encourage and structure discussions around issues that matter to the team, thus creating engagement through acknowledgment. Websites like Retromat offer hundreds of different games and exercises to make retrospectives enjoyable and valuable for the whole team.

There is no single solution, and consequently no single correct answer, to either boredom or this question. What's important is that your candidate acknowledges that boredom with routine might become an issue and that there are ways to deal with it.

Read more: "How to Curate Retrospectives for Fun and Profit With Retromat."

Read more: "Retrospective Anti-Patterns."

Question 37

SET 5: RETROSPECTIVES   83

If your team is picking reasonable action items but not delivering, how would you address the situation?

During a retrospective, the members of a scrum team are usually expected to pick a series of action items (tasks to be done). If these action items are subsequently not completed promptly, the scrum master needs to follow up.

A team might not be completing the action items they've picked because they've run into an external impediment. If this is the case, the scrum master must address the cause, and the team can then catch up during a later sprint. However, if there is no external impediment, the problem is likely due to motivation, attitude, or personal issues within the team. In this latter case, the scrum master needs to provide the offending team members with sufficient encouragement or motivation to overcome the problem — and then see that they deliver on their commitments.

If a team is not completing the action items they've picked and the problem ultimately cannot be resolved, choosing action items becomes a useless exercise and the team will suffer as a result.

Question 38

How would you recommend following up on action items?

A scrum master is expected to follow up on the action items (tasks to be done) that members of a scrum team pick during their team's retrospectives. A good way for a scrum master to do this is to start talking about the status of the action items picked during the last retrospective before picking new ones by initiating a discussion at the beginning of each new retrospective. If this discussion uncovers that action items picked during a previous retrospective haven't yet been completed as expected, the team needs to understand why — and prevent it from happening again.

[1] Mad Sad Glad is a retrospective exercise designed to elicit feedback and possible corrective actions.

[2] SMART is a mnemonic for various acronyms that provide guidelines to be used during the process of setting goals.

[3] This is the format described in the book Agile Retrospectives: Making Good Teams Great by Diana Larsen and Esther Derby.

Set 6: Agile Metrics

Background

- The purpose of metrics, generally, is to understand a current situation better and gain insight on how it's likely to change over time.
- A metric is a leading indicator for a pattern, providing an opportunity to analyze the cause of change — and act appropriately in due course.
- Metrics in an agile context are not used to manage, and certainly not micromanage, an individual (particularly the creative worker) — contrary to traditional command-and-control management structures.
- Metrics in an agile organization should be used to provide the scrum team — agile practitioners all — with insights on how to continuously improve, helping them achieve their goals.
- Agile practitioners strive for autonomy, mastery, and purpose as explained by Daniel Pink.
- Agile practitioners address personal development with metrics by applying methods like Objectives and Key Results (OKR).
- The experienced agile practitioner realizes that autonomy

and accountability are equally crucial for self-organized scrum teams. Without metrics, both autonomy and accountability are limited.

- The metrics most suitable to agile reflect either a team's progress in becoming agile or the organization's progress in becoming a learning organization.
- Both qualitative and quantitative metrics may be used for agile:
  - Qualitative metrics typically reveal more than quantitative metrics when applied to the scrum team.
  - Quantitative metrics provide more insight than qualitative metrics when applied to the organization.
- Any metric used for agile must be tailored to the organization.
- The metrics that the scrum master should be tracking are only those that apply to the scrum team. Metrics that measure the individual should be ignored.
- A metric's context should always be recorded to avoid misinterpretation.
- Parameters that are easy to follow should not be measured for that reason alone — especially if a report is readily available in the project management software being used.

Question 39

Are there any standard metrics that you would track? If so, which, and for what purpose?

When tracking metrics at the organizational level, the effects

SET 6: AGILE METRICS

of any process or change can be measured quantitatively with a **metrics scoring model**. The measured impacts would include:

- the ability to respond to change and produce valuable code (e.g., the capacity to break down features);
- the duality of planning at both release and sprint;
- the flexibility to adapt to changing facts, time boxes, and continuous delivery;
- the frequency with which scrum teams are bidding on stories, and whether the teams are exercising any freedom in their approach to solving them;
- the creation and growth of a culture of shared learning; and
- the continuity with which features are delivered.

The design of a metrics scoring model should take into account the agile maturity of the organization such that qualitative aspects may be quantified, and thus compared. If the metrics scoring model can be designed before introducing an agile framework into an organization, the status quo should be surveyed to establish a baseline against which to measure these effects and track their evolution over time.

Any metrics used to measure the effects of a relevant process or change should regularly be recorded, throughout the agile journey. Surveying the members of an organization's scrum teams is a good start.

Question 40

Your scrum team is consistently failing to meet commitments, and their velocity is volatile. What are the

most probable reasons for this problem, and how would you address it with the team?

If a scrum team is exhibiting a volatile velocity and consistently failing to meet their commitments, it suggests that velocity is being used as the common metric for measuring that team's progress. Your candidate should mention this, and talk about the notoriety of 'velocity' as the industry's most prevalent metric for measuring a team's progress. They should further be able to explain why velocity is altogether a doubtful agile metric and point out that quantitative metrics are not ideally suited to measuring a team's progress in mastering scrum.

Many factors make a scrum team's velocity volatile:

- New team members being educated;
- Experienced members leaving the team;
- The team working in uncharted territory;
- The team working with legacy code, probably undocumented;
- The team running into unexpected technical debt;
- Holidays and sick leave reducing the team's capacity;
- An executive intervention changing a sprint's scope; and
- The team is addressing priority bugs.

Another common cause for a scrum team to consistently fail in meeting their commitments is that the team's commitments are frequently too aggressive. This might indicate that the user stories are being poorly prepared (e.g., not meeting the team's definition of ready), thus making the stories difficult for the team to estimate. Conversely, the projects being given the team might suffer from poorly documented legacy code, excessive

SET 6: AGILE METRICS

technical debt, or just too much buggy and poorly written code — all of which make estimation a gamble.

Your candidate should not align themselves with the fallacy that an agile adoption is working only because a scrum team's commitment and velocity are aligned. Cooking the agile books is easy to do!

Read more: "Scrum: The Obsession with Commitment Matching Velocity."

Question 41

What qualitative agile metrics would you consider tracking?

The purpose of qualitative metrics in agile is to gain insight into how one or more of an organization's scrum teams are progressing with agile.

There are several self-assessment tests available that a scrum team can regularly run to collect qualitative metrics about their implementation of scrum — the Scrum Checklist by Henrik Kniberg is a good example. The interval to test via self-assessment is every 4–12 weeks, with teams of lesser maturity running their tests at the lower end of this range. The individual values recorded by these tests are not very important, but the trend over time is. To visualize these patterns, a scrum master will need to aggregate the results — in the case of Henrik Kniberg's checklist, an agile practice map [1] may be created over time.

While self-assessment tests like Henrik Kniberg's checklist are usually team exercises for recording **implementation** metrics, **sentiment** metrics are best captured by running anonymous opinion polls to ensure the participation of the more introverted team members. Using opinion polls, typical questions for recording sentiment metrics include

- What value did the team deliver in the last sprint?
- Has the level of technical debt increased or decreased during the last sprint?
- Are you happy working with your teammates?
- Would you recommend your employer (or client) to a friend seeking a new job?

It's best to run opinion polls after every sprint; these surveys should only require a few seconds to complete. As with the self-assessment tests, the individual values recorded by running anonymous opinion polls are not very important — it's the trend over time that matters. Trends derived from these polls are great points for discussion during a team's retrospectives.

Concerning metrics in general, your candidate should support the Agile Manifesto and its principle of transparency: all metrics should be available to all members of a scrum team, and largely also to those working in the product delivery organization [2] generally.

Read more: "Agile Metrics — The Good, the Bad, and the Ugly."

[1] An agile practice map consists of a user story mapping practice to avoid a failure made of incremental delivery.

[2] A product delivery organization is essentially everyone

SET 6: AGILE METRICS

within an organization who's involved with getting a product to market.

Set 7: How to Kick-off a Transition to Scrum

Background

- There is no checklist or master plan readily available, or that could be made readily available, that would ensure a successful transition to Scrum.
- The 'best practices' of and 'lessons learned' by other organizations during their transition to scrum may indicate a direction to take when transitioning, though the context of their change may not be comparable: what worked for Spotify may not work for General Motors.
- Every transition to scrum should start with understanding the 'why': why should the organization become agile?
- Reasons typically given by management for transitioning to scrum and other agile practices include:
  - Making the organization more efficient;
  - Helping the organization deliver faster; and
  - Improving the predictability of delivery dates.
- The recognized benefits of transitioning to scrum and other agile practices are:

- Outperforming competitors by creating a learning organization;
- Creating a great workplace culture by providing room for autonomy, mastery, and purpose; and
- Mastering continuous product discovery and delivery (thus minimizing risk).

- Agile and its benefits need to be sold to an organization before beginning its transition to scrum — agile is not everybody's darling, and personal agendas will be affected by a successful change.
- A transition to scrum will encounter inertia and resistance to change directly proportional to the size of the organization.
- How a transition to scrum should be undertaken depends upon many factors, including an organization's industry, regulations and compliance rules, the size and age of the organization, workplace culture, the maturity of an organization's products and services, team size, and current project management practices.
- How a transition to scrum is undertaken should be determined by the goals of the organization — what is hoped to be achieved.
- A successful transition to scrum requires the backing of C-level executives; a bottom-up approach is futile.
- The first step of any transition to scrum is the creation of the first scrum team.
- Transitioning to scrum requires training and educating the entire organization — not just future scrum team members — in agile practices and principles. Training and education are essential for a successful transition.
- There is a huge difference between 'doing Agile' and 'being

agile.' Transitioning to scrum successfully means becoming — and being — agile.

- In an organization transitioning to scrum, future scrum masters should be agents of change rather than drill sergeants — this is by design, given their lack of proper authority.
- Creating a 'happy agile island' for the product and engineering department is a valid objective. However, in comparison to breaking up functional silos and creating a learning organization, it is likely to deliver a lesser return on investment.

Question 42

How would you prepare to kick off a transition to scrum?

If you don't know where you are going, any road will get you there. Your candidate should understand that an agile transition needs to have an objective and a goal — which means planning.

To prepare for kicking off a transition to scrum is to listen and observe: your candidate should express interest in interviewing as many team members and stakeholders as possible, before jumping into action. These interviews should include everyone, no matter their role — engineers, QA professionals [1], UX and UI designers, product managers — to identify the patterns underlying current problems, failures, and dysfunction within the organization. Merging those trends with the most pressing technical and business issues will determine the most likely objectives for the first scrum teams. This observation phase, during which a scrum master performs their interviews, will typically require between four and eight weeks depending on the size and structure of the organization.

The training of future team members and stakeholders should commence and run parallel to the interviews. Creating the first scrum teams from the existing engineering and product departments is the second step in kicking off a transition to scrum. The candidate should be able to sketch the rough plan of a transition and address common issues that might arise during kickoff.

Read more: "How to Kick-off Your Agile Transition."

Question 43

How would you create the first scrum team?

When an organization is transitioning to scrum and at the same time dealing with significant organizational, business, and technical problems, the founding members of its scrum teams should be volunteers who fully understand the challenge ahead of them, rather than people pressed into service. The best volunteers are those eager to prove that becoming agile is the most effective way to reach an objective.

Candidates for the role of scrum master should be astute enough to suggest inviting every member of the product delivery team, as well as the C-level executives sponsoring the transition, to a kickoff meeting. The objective of a transition kickoff meeting is to support the members of the engineering and product teams in how they choose to self-organize into the first cross-functional scrum teams. Transition kickoff meetings can last a few hours or several days, depending upon the circumstances of a particular organization.

Despite the importance of the kickoff meeting to a scrum transition, going much deeper into its structure will take too much time from the interview. It's more important that your candidates present a brief roadmap of what should happen next for the newly formed scrum teams.

Although somewhat dependent upon the existing skills, experience, and training of the members of an organization's new scrum teams, your candidates should anticipate having to teach the very basics of scrum following a kickoff meeting. They might propose doing this through a series of workshops or on-the-job training with exercises in product backlog refinement, writing user stories, estimating, and creating offline boards.

Question 44

What do you recommend a newly formed scrum team works on first?

The first critical issue for the majority of newly formed scrum teams is the existing legacy product backlog. Answers to this question need not reference Tuckman's team development stages (see Question 28), additional team building exercises, or any form of scrum training or workshop not concerned with the product backlog.

It is a rare occasion for a scrum master to start from scratch with a brand new team and no existing product — even more so in a nascent organization like a startup. Most often, it's an existing product delivery organization with existing products and services who will 'go agile.' For these cases, your candidate should point out that refining the legacy product backlog is the practical first step.

The legacy product backlog per se is an interesting artifact because it provides comprehensive insight into the product delivery organization's history: this particular backlog allows for identifying organizational debt, process insufficiencies, questionable product decisions, and other anti-patterns. Looking at a legacy product backlog, an excellent candidate will be able to point out some of these anti-patterns (e.g. outdated or poorly maintained tickets), and provide a good idea about how to transform the legacy backlog into a well-refined, current product backlog such that a new scrum team (including the product owner) could work with.

Candidates should mention that running a product backlog refinement workshop creates a good opportunity to provide a new scrum team and product owner hands-on training with scrum. This is because a backlog refinement workshop will typically cover user story creation, knowledge transfer among team members, the estimation process (if applicable), introductory agile metrics, technical debt analysis, and other topics critical to scrum.

Read more: "Product Backlog Refinement."

[1] Quality assurance professionals focus on quality earlier in the development process during defect prevention.

Set 8: Scrum Anti-Patterns

Background

- Humans are fallible, so with this propensity for error, there will always be room for (professional) improvement – including scrum masters.
- Anti-patterns will emerge when core principles (as laid out in the Manifesto for Agile Software Development and the Scrum Guide) are ignored, made to fit existing structures, or watered down.
- The deterioration of principles may be a deliberate process (creating a form of cargo cult agile), unintentional, or a result of good intentions applied in the wrong way.
- Whatever the deterioration process, emerging anti-patterns will prevent an organization from reaping the benefits of agile software development.
- Recognizing Scrum and agile anti-patterns is therefore fundamental in the effort for serious, continuous improvement.
- Anti-patterns can be identified by observation, retrospectives, and other forms of feedback generating activities.

Read More: The "Scrum Anti-Patterns Guide" is another free ebook from the Hands-On Agile series of practical guides from the trenches. It covers more than 160 of the scrum anti-patterns.

Question 45

Which scrum master anti-patterns do you know of that can happen during a sprint?

Typical scrum master sprint anti-patterns are below. Any of these behaviors will impede the team's productivity. The scrum master must prevent them from manifesting themselves:

- **Flow disruption**: The scrum master allows stakeholders to disrupt the workflow of the development team during the sprint. (There are several possibilities on how stakeholders can interrupt the flow of the team during a sprint:
    - The scrum master has a laissez-faire policy regarding access to the development team.
    - The scrum master does not object when management invites engineers to random meetings as subject matter experts.
    - Lastly, the scrum master allows either the stakeholders or managers to turn the daily scrum into a reporting session.)
- **Lack of support**: The scrum master does not support team members who need help with a task. (Development teams often create tasks an engineer can finish within a day. However, if someone struggles with a task for more than two days without voicing that they need support, the scrum

SET 8: SCRUM ANTI-PATTERNS

master should address the issue. Importantly, this is also the reason for marking tasks on a physical board with red dots each day if they haven't been moved on to the next column.)

- **Micromanagement**: The scrum master does not prevent the product owner – or anyone else – from assigning tasks to engineers. (The development team organizes itself typically without external intervention. And the scrum master should act as the shield of the team in this respect.)

- **#NoRetro**: The scrum master does not gather data during the sprint that would support the team in the upcoming retrospective. (This is self-explanatory.)

Question 46

What anti-patterns do you know of that can happen during a retrospective?

Typical scrum retrospective anti-patterns:

- **Waste of time**: The team does not collectively value the retrospective. (If some team members consider the retrospective to be of little or no value, it is most often the retrospective itself that sucks. Is it the same procedure every time, ritualized and boring? Have a meta-retrospective on the retrospective itself. Change the venue. Have a beer- or wine-driven retrospective. There are so many things a scrum master can do to make retrospectives exciting and valuable again, reducing the absence rate. Furthermore, it is good to remember that (in my experience) introverts like to take part in retrospectives also.)

- **Prisoners**: Some team members only participate because they are forced to team up. (Don't pressure anyone to take part in a retrospective. Instead, make it worth their time. The drive to continuously improve as a team needs to be fueled by intrinsic motivation, neither by fear nor by order. Tip: Retromat's "Why are you here?" exercise is a good opener for a retrospective from time to time.)

- **Groundhog day**: The retrospective never changes in composition, venue, or length. (In this case, the is that the team will revisit the same issues over and over again – it's like groundhog day without the happy ending.)

- **Let's have it next sprint**: The team postpones the retrospective into the next sprint. (Beyond the "inspect & adapt" task, the retrospective serves as a moment of closure, helping reset everybody's mind so that the team can focus on the upcoming sprint goal. That is the reason why we have the retrospective before the planning of the follow-up sprint. Postponing it into the next sprint may also interrupt the flow of the team, and delay tackling possible improvements by up to a sprint. This is why it is important to have the retrospective before the planning of the follow-up sprint.)

- **#NoDocumentation**: No one is taking minutes for later use. (A retrospective is a substantial investment for many reasons and should be taken seriously. Taking notes and photos supports the process.)

- **No psychological safety**: The retrospective is an endless cycle of blame and finger-pointing. (The team wins together, the team loses together. Unfortunately, the blame game documents both the failure of the scrum master as the facilitator of the retrospective as well as the team's lack of maturity and communication skills.)

- **Bullying**: One or two team members are dominating the retrospective. (This communication behavior is often a sign of either a weak or uninterested scrum master. The retrospective needs to be a safe place where everyone–introverts included–can address issues and provide their feedback free from team members who are dominating the conversation, bullying or intimidating other teammates. The failure to provide a safe place will result in participants dropping out of the retrospective and render the results obsolete. It is the main responsibility of the scrum master to ensure that everyone can be heard and has an opportunity to voice their thoughts. According to Google, equally distributed speaking time fosters and signifies a high-performing team. **Read More**: "What Google Learned From Its Quest to Build the Perfect Team").

- **Stakeholder alert**: Stakeholders participate in the retrospective. (There are plenty of scrum ceremonies that address the communication needs of stakeholders: the sprint review, the product backlog refinement, the daily scrums – not to mention opportunities of having a conversation at water coolers, over coffee, or during lunchtime. If that spectrum of possibilities is still not sufficient, feel free to have additional meetings. However, the retrospective is off-limits to stakeholders.)

- **Passivity**: The team members are present but are not participating. (There are plenty of reasons for such a behavior: they regard the retrospective a waste of time, it is an unsafe place, or the participants are bored to death by its predictiveness. The team members may also fear negative repercussions should they be absent, or maybe a homogenous group of introverts was unwittingly hired. Whatever the reason, there is likely no quick fix. The scrum master needs to determine what style of retrospective will work best in their organization's context.)

Question 47

How can you (as a scrum master) identify where you need to improve?

This is a simple question: Regularly ask your team and stakeholders how you can improve as a scrum master.

Why not run a retrospective on yourself? A dedicated retrospective is much more effective than spending five minutes, asking for hints at how you might improve, at the end of each regular team retrospective.

Conclusion (Advice for the Hiring Organization)

During the interview, move as fast as possible from the theoretical to the practical. Be careful not to waste too much time discussing the advantages of agile methodologies or other (likely) opinionated topics. Two or three questions from each of the sets in this handbook will provide more than enough ground for an engaging sixty-minute conversation.

Scrum has always been a hands-on business, so your candidate will need to have a passion for getting their hands dirty if they're going to be successful. Although the rules are basic, building a capable team from a group of individuals with different backgrounds, levels of engagement, and personal agendas is a complex task – as is often the case when people and communication are involved.

The larger an organization and more levels of management, the more likely there will be resistance or possibly even failure when applying agile. In these circumstances, it would be wise to choose the pragmatic veteran, who has experienced failure at other organizations (and may carry the scars to prove it), over a junior scrum master.

Being a Certified ScrumMaster® — or having any such kind of designation — does not guarantee success. (Certified ScrumMaster® is a registered trademark of Scrum Alliance, Inc.)

PART IV

THE TRIAL DAY: CHECKING THE CHEMISTRY

The trial day — the final part of the match-making journey.

No matter, if they offer you a contract shortly after the interview, I do recommend to have a trial day anyway. While organizations and people usually manage to present the best side of them during an interview of one or two hours, it is hardly possible to preserve the same level over the course of a day when you are involved in the operational business.

You will get a first-hand experience on the culture, the people, the processes, and — most important — numerous anti-patterns of all kinds. Don't waste the opportunity.

Preparing for Your Trial Day

Why a Trial Day is a Great Opportunity

So, you have made it successfully through the initial interview round(s), and already met with people from the Human Resource and management teams. You may also have met some of your prospective new colleagues during the interviews, received an office tour, or had the opportunity to check out the cantina.

In the past, this custom might have been sufficient for the organization to offer a job, though, at present, it is more likely that the organization will invite the candidate on a trial day, or week, to work with the prospective team on real product development issues.

Personally, a trial day represents an excellent opportunity for the candidate to make an informed decision whether or not to work for the organization in question. A trial day/week allows you to discover the inner workings of the organization, and gain an unfiltered impression of the organization's culture, its agile mindset (or lack of it), as well as many of the protagonists. It also provides an opportunity to get a first-hand impression of the working environment. Finally, the lunch break is an excellent occasion to interact with and observe the prospective teammates in a more extended, social context.

Therefore, if a company should offer you a contract without a trial day/week, you may undoubtedly suggest and discuss having one. Ultimately, this small effort could save you from the distress of making the wrong decision.

Note: Trial days that a suitable organization or employer offers are typically compensated at a fair rate. If the organization states that they expect participation in such an effort without offering remuneration, this should raise a red flag.

Why Trial Days Are a Good Sign for the State of Agile in the Organization

Shortly, all creative, technology-based organizations will need to abandon the command and control structures that have heretofore served the industrial world of the 20th century so well.

Instead, they will need to become self-organized structures, built around autonomous teams. (Consider reading General Stanley McChrystal: "Team of Teams: New Rules of Engagement for a Complex World.")

Note: An excellent introduction to ununderstanding he "Team of Teams" from an organizational point of view, is Culture First's podcast: "Team of Thrones."

In such an agile world, recruiting will now become a team

decision, and the role of the human resources department will change into a supportive one. Recruiters will need to become servant leaders or facilitators in the peer recruiting process, because the teams will determine, by working with someone on real problems, as to whether they desire a particular candidate to join them.

You may question why this change of process will be required in the first place. There are plenty of good, consequential reasons for the change, and these are my top three:

1. An autonomous team is empowered to make decisions that directly impact the return on (product) investment. On the other hand, any decision by HR and a manager on new teammates – without including the team – might be found to be patronizing.
2. An autonomous team has skin in the game by assuming the responsibility of making a recruiting decision. Thereby, they are motivated to go the extra mile to make the new connection work.
3. An autonomous team is immediately involved in the recruitment process; if not, it should signal to all candidates that the organization is not agile, merely "doing Agile," which is a weak value proposition in the war for talent with an agile mindset.

Read More: "Peer Recruiting: How to Hire a Scrum Master in Agile Times."

Jerks Always Out Themselves

Another good reason for a trial day/week is that while a lot of jerks are good at concealing their true nature during interviews, they will always out themselves in a typical working situation.

When a jerk joins the team for even a day in the working environment, it will be noticed that they will find no further need to keep up the I-have-to-be-nice façade which camouflaged their true nature during the interview phase.

Read More: "Your Company Culture Is Who You Hire, Fire & Promote."

Why Research Prepares for Trial Day

You will greatly benefit on the trial day by any knowledge gathered through extending your research to all participants and team members involved in your trial day. The preparation for a trial day at the team or staff level is not much different from preparation made for the interview session earlier in the process.

In addition to the staff research, you will want to familiarize yourself with the organization: its market, competitors, general technological trends, opportunities, and challenges. It is also wise to familiarize yourself with the financial standing of the organization by reading any financial reports.

Staff Research

It is essential to learn in advance who will be participating in your trial day. Usually, the candidate will meet and work with the team that is looking for a Scrum master, instead of being passed from one scrum team to another.

If you are not provided with a list of the participants in advance, ask for it. There is no reason to withhold the information from you. If they claim confidentiality reasons, suggest signing the typically required non-disclosure agreement in advance so they can provide you with the list.

Once you know the names of the team members you will meet, make sure to research them properly. Ask yourself: Are some of them speaking for the organization at conferences or meetups? Are team members blogging, hosting a podcast, and the like? (See above.)

Tools

Have you ever met a craftsman without a toolbox? Probably not.

Bringing your tools to the trial day is not just a question of pride in your craftsmanship, it is also a necessity. Never expect that the organization will provide you with the tools of your craft in either adequate quality or quantity. No matter which organization invites you on a trial day, always come fully prepared and bring your gear: markers, crayons, stickies, or planning poker cards. Bringing your gear signals professionalism to the trial day participants and may very well save the day, too.

My suggested standard toolset comprises of several Neuland markers and extra sticky post-its in different colors and sizes, as well as a large box of wax coloring blocks. Also, it is helpful to bring pencils or markers for the participants.

Retrospectives

Another field that deserves attention in advance of a trial day is retrospectives. These are favorite tasks for trial days, and hence should be treated seriously. The minimum level of preparation is to choose a set of exercises that might apply to the team's situation. My recommendation is to prepare for three different retrospective lengths: 30 minutes, 60 minutes, and 90 minutes.

Usually, Retromat is an excellent place to prepare retrospectives because it outlines the five stages: from setting the stage, gathering data, generating insights, deciding what to do, to closing the retrospective. (Find examples of the different retrospective lengths in the chapter *Possible Exercises During a Trial D*ay.)

Should you draw retrospective exercises in advance? This would indeed save time during the trial day and might add another layer of professionalism from the organization's point of view. On the other hand, if you have decent drawing skills, doing this in front of your prospective teammates leaves quite an impression (provided paper is available).

Print Questionnaires and Bring Your WiFi

If you intend to use printed questionnaires to get up to speed (as in the "Cargo Cult Checklist"), I suggest that you print them in advance and bring them with you. Do not expect that you can access the organization's local printers. This also applies to Internet access. To be on the safe side, make sure that your hotspot is working.

Bring some Slide Decks

Finally, you should have some slide decks available that cover the most critical issues of agile software development:

- Product backlog refinement,
- User stories creation,
- Slicing of user stories,
- User story estimation, and
- Scrum ceremonies (sprint review, sprint planning, sprint retrospective.)

Getting Started on Trial Day

Be Punctual

Most of the time, a trial day will be just that – a single day. Given this restriction, its schedule will be tightly packed, with little slack time. Being late is not an option. I recommend reducing your stress level by adequately preparing your trip in advance. Just apply common sense and fight your hard-wired need to procrastinate until the last minute.

Note: Creating a list of your observations during the trial will be helpful for the wrap-up session at the end of the trial day.

Observing the Workplace and the Surroundings

During the initial interview, there is not much time to gain the necessary insight into the working environment of the organization. Usually, but not always, you will get a guided, overview tour of the organization's facility. A trial day, however, brings the true colors of the workspace to light so to speak.

In addition to meeting your prospective teammates, the trial day also offers a unique insight into the workspace of the team. By workspace, I am referring to those elements which help an agile team succeed – often entirely different from those perceived by management or interior designers.

The Office Space

Things to watch out for at the facility level:

1. Is the Scrum team co-located, or scattered over several floors within the building? The latter is negatively affecting the Scrum team's effectiveness. It is also a sign that the organization might still be ensconced in a project mindset (where project teams are created temporarily to be split up again after the project's completion). Contrary to this, all agile practitioners advocate investing in the longevity of teams, and co-locating the team members is the first step. For example, IBM is now considering it innovative to abandon remote work in favor of implementing co-location of teams. https://qz.com/924167/ibm-remote-work-pioneer-is-calling-thousands-of-employees-back-to-the-office/)
2. Does the office have an open floor plan? Are the majority of people wearing headphones? Do they prefer working from home? Open floor plans are often considered to be the ideal agile workspace by nurturing collaboration and keeping everyone in the loop with spreading news and information. However, a lot of creative workers feel that the noise and sound level often accompanying open floor plans challenges their need for concentration, deep work, and flow. Additionally, agile teams require more defined

spaces to create a sense of team togetherness, not just any area within an open space. (**Read More:** "Just shut up and let your devs concentrate, advises Stack Overflow CEO Joel Spolsky.")
3. Is there a decent meeting room, or playground available for teamwork? An absence indicates a lack of suitable workspace. Agile practices need different types of workspaces to be fully effective. Agile requires:

    1. A space for collaborating with small teams of 2 to maybe 5 or 6 people,
    2. A silent workspace to for deep, focused work,
    3. A space for informal, ad hoc meetings of 2 to 3 people,
    4. A large, flexible meeting room – or better yet, a playground, where one or several teams can work together (as in a sprint review meeting), and
    5. Social spaces (like cafés) which encourage informal networking and the possibility of a serendipitous meeting with someone interesting.

If all or any of these requirements are missing, it indicates that the organization has not yet learned that becoming agile also requires investments at the facility level. The agile workspace is no longer a cubicle-dominated assembly line of white-collar workers:

1. Are there sufficient whiteboards available? Most walls within the workspace of an agile organization should by default have whiteboards to encourage instant collaboration. Brick or glass walls may be aesthetically pleasing, but without whiteboards, they impede the agile transition by prohibiting spontaneous collaboration.
2. Are there any information radiators other than the

physical boards of the Scrum teams? This taps into the question of how the organization is handling transparency. Are there any visible performance dashboards aggregating data or information (e.g., the number of sign-ups of new, paying customers, current revenue metrics, NPS scores, a list of hypotheses to be tested, the dates of the next user-tests) indicating how well the application is doing? If these are missing, the organization is still struggling with a vital component of all agile practices: transparency on relevant information for everyone. (Keep in mind the possibility that the organization may have just started its agile transition or have compliance rules preventing this practice. As always, life is neither black, nor white, but gray.)

Read More: "Agile Workspace: The Undervalued Success Factor."

The Team Workspace

Once you move on to the team area, look for the following:

1. Does the co-located (not virtual) team have a physical board? If so, what does the board look like and possibly signify? Physical boards come in all shapes and sizes. Some are properly set up, others are improvised, and utilize what the workspace provides. If boards are actively used it signals improvisation and a good agile mindset within the team, that may not happen to be met by the organization. (In this case, ask for how long the

improvisation has been going on.) Physical boards that are not adequately used, and only display outdated tickets or sprint dates, or lack some advanced features such as parking lots, indicate a more severe problem. If this usage is team-based, great. This might be your future job. If it truthfully has an organizational cause, this should be noted on your list of observations. (**Read More:** "How to Build Offline Boards.")
2. How do you perceive the atmosphere within the team area? Is it a likable place when you walk in? Or, is Dilbert smiling at you from all corners of the team area? The latter is often a sign for either a dysfunctional team or dysfunctional communication between the team and the rest of the organization. Try to understand possible issues by a query and addressing them.
3. What are office supplies noticeably available? This may sound trivial, but my personal experience has shown that the availability of office supplies often directly reflects the organization's agile mindset. Is there just one color of cheap, small-sized stickies? This might indicate that the organization has a long way to go before it becomes agile.

What do you notice that is beyond the Scrum basics, such as Kudo cards or the results of a delegation poker session? This is not so much about noticing Management 3.0 artifacts. Instead, it is about anything that might reveal that the team has started moving beyond the usual Scrum mechanics and is no longer confusing Scrum with being agile. Also, acknowledging their co-workers' contributions or outsourcing decisions to the leadership are both encouraging signs of such a development.

The General Impression of the Office Space

In addition to the functions of the (previously referred to as) "agile workspace," observations in the rest of the office can provide more insight. Here are several:

- Are the organization's values printed and posted on the walls?
- Is there litter on the floor? Even more telling is whether people are picking it up?
- What is the state of the bathrooms? Are there any cartoons posted on how to use a toilet brush correctly? Well, if so, then it was probably necessary to point this out.
- How do the kitchens look? Are they tidy, or are they filled with used coffee mugs because people are too occupied, lazy, or just not caring enough to place them in the dishwasher? Personally, any lofty behavior or attitude displayed in even this manner does not align itself with an agile mindset.
- Are people easily chatting with each other?
- Are there dogs at the office? A lot of dog-friendly organizations are no command and control-style organizations.
- Are regular employees treating the support staff with respect?
- Are people personalizing their desks with plants or photos?

Be aware that there are a lot of small hints all over an office that will provide you with additional clues for identifying certain issues regarding the organization. All you have to do is look out for them.

Meet the Team and Get up to Speed

Time Is at a Premium

Starting a new job as Scrum master or agile coach usually begins with listening to people and observing how things are done. This period easily takes up to four weeks. During a trial day, that luxury of time is not afforded you.

However, there is a helpful trial-day version of this process: come prepared with questionnaires for both the product owner, as well as the scrum team.

Getting up to Speed by Asking the Product Owner

The first set of questions addresses the collaboration between the product owner and the scrum team. The questions have been modeled on the fundamental principles that high-performing teams have in common:

1. What are the product vision and the related go-to-market strategy?
2. How do you learn about new ideas and requirements?
3. How do you include user research in the product discovery process?
4. How much time do you allocate to user research and understanding your customers' needs?
5. At what stage do you involve the scrum team in the product discovery process?
6. How do you organize the collaboration with stakeholders?
7. How do you deal with pet projects?
8. What is your approach to creating product roadmaps?
9. How large is your product backlog?
10. What is the typical age of a user story in the product backlog?
11. What is your average lead time from picking an idea for validation to adding the corresponding user story to the product backlog?
12. Does your product backlog contain user stories that none of the current team members is familiar with?
13. How often are you grooming the product backlog?
14. How many user stories are you working on in parallel during backlog grooming?
15. How long does the grooming of a typical user story take?
16. How are you creating user stories? (Is it a joint team effort?)
17. How are you discussing user stories? (For example, only during grooming sessions, or also on Slack or via comments on tickets?)
18. Are you changing user stories once they become an item of a sprint backlog?
19. When do you accept user stories?
20. Have you ever rejected user stories?

You can download a PDF of the questionnaire here: "20 Questions from New Scrum Master to Product Owner."

Read More: Marty Cagan's post 'Product Success.'

Getting up to Speed by Asking "Your Team"

The trial day provides the opportunity to ask the team members about the flavor of agile they are practicing, and I strongly suggest that you ask the empirical questions. It cannot just be about gathering information on practices and the organization's processes.

It also has to be about having a first glimpse at team dynamics: Can you discern as to whether the team is already a team, or just merely a group of people that happens to be in the same place at the same time? Is the team cross-functional? Who is speaking and how often? Are some team members silent, or is the air-time in discussions evenly distributed? Asking questions about how the team is collaborating may also reveal opposing opinions, tensions, or even conflicts among team members.

Choosing ten to fifteen questions from the following list will easily support a 30-minute to a 45-minute discussion:

1. How large is your product backlog?
2. What is the typical age of a user story in the product backlog?
3. What is your average lead time from an idea being added to the product backlog to its delivery?

4. Does your product backlog contain user stories that none of the current team members is familiar with?
5. How often are you refining the product backlog?
6. How many user stories are you working on in parallel during backlog refinement?
7. How long does the refinement of a typical user story take?
8. How are you creating user stories? (Is it a joint team effort with the product owner, or is the PO writing the user stories and the team estimates them?)
9. Where are you discussing user stories? (For example, only during refinement sessions, or also on Slack or via comments on tickets?)
10. Do you apply a definition of ready (DoR) standard to your user stories?
11. If so, of what criteria is your DoR composed?
12. Who is writing acceptance criteria and in what format?
13. How are you estimating the effort applied to a user story?
14. Do you estimate effort applied by using staff-hours or story points?
15. How do you use this estimation process if the team should share different opinions?
16. What is a typical distribution of story sizes in your sprint backlogs?
17. Are you re-estimating user stories at the end of a sprint? If so, under which circumstances are you doing so?
18. What was the average velocity of the last three sprints?
19. How many user stories are typically not finished within a sprint (and for what reasons)?
20. Are you changing user stories once they become an item of a sprint backlog? If so, under what circumstances?
21. What are the obstacles the team is facing today?
22. What are any dependencies on other teams?
23. Define and discuss at least three key team goals for a current project or product.

24. What are the critical success factors needed to achieve our team goals?
25. What do team members hope to achieve with this project?
26. What type of work environment do we want to create during this project?
27. What can we do as a team to ensure we support each other to achieve our team goals?
28. What should we do when we are not achieving our goals because of not supporting each other?
29. How should we celebrate success in achieving our goals?

Note: You can download and take this printable version with you to the interview: "20 Questions a New Scrum Master Should Ask Her Team to Get up to Speed."

Watch: "Goal Summit 2016: The Science Behind Effective Teams at Google." (Google's vice president of people operations, Prasad Setty, dives into Google's best practices and recent research on the driving forces behind team effectiveness.)

Possible Exercises During a Trial Day

Build an Offline Board

Building an offline board is a team task. Nevertheless, it is also a favorite scrum master exercise during interviews or trial days. The rationale behind this is simple: how could a scrum master guide a team in the right direction to improve a board if they cannot create one on their own?

Offline boards vary from team to team, affected by the culture of the organization, the maturity of the product, team size, policies, and various other factors. There are, however, some basic components that are beneficial for all teams:

- Display all policies affecting the work (like the working agreement, or both the DoR [definition of ready] and DoD [definition of done]).
- Display a schedule for all ceremonies: when and where does the team gather for stand-ups, product backlog refinements and sprint planning sessions, sprint reviews, and the team retrospective?

- Provide all pertinent information on the sprint, including the sprint goal.
- Organize the sprint backlog: all issues in the sprint backlog must be prioritized. (Have the team choose their style: it should be systematic, either from top to bottom, or from left to right — as long as it is orderly, and works for the team, it cannot be wrong.)
- Create issue lanes, with only one issue per lane. (Tip: Limiting the space of the lanes to the size of your index cards or stickies will automatically create a work-in-progress limit.)
- Set up all workflow stages contingent upon the team's workflow.
- Consider adding an express lane for issues that (were not picked for the current sprint but) require the immediate attention of the team. (Tip: Setting up an express lane requires a strict code defining its use. If not specified, stakeholders may attempt to push for a lot of issues to be placed in the express lane.)
- Ensure that a list of the do-not-disturb hours is visible.
- Display an availability chart: who is available during the current sprint?
- Finally, add some board art (and why not start with the team logo).

The offline board exercise may also help determine whether an analog solution (based on index cards and a whiteboard) might be an adequate substitution for a software tool such as Jira.

Instead of creating an offline board from scratch, the candidate may also be asked to analyze an existing board and point out its shortcomings. Here are some anti-patterns of offline boards:

- Some issues of the current sprint are not represented by a card on the board.
- Cards are not moved to reflect their current status, thus obscuring the team's real progress.
- Cards are neither initialed, nor with an avatar attached to them, so it is unknown who is working on the issue.
- Tasks that take longer than a day are not marked. (This raises a lot of questions, for example: Does someone need help? Has the problem already been addressed during a stand-up? Was the team disrupted during the sprint?)
- There is no work-in-progress limit applied: this can lead to too much work in development, or too many issues piling up in the code review and QA section. (Admittedly, developers are also cherry-picking.)

Read More: "How to Build Offline Boards – Agile Transition (Part 3)."

Creating Concepts

This "creating concepts" chapter bundles several tests and exercises during which a candidate can demonstrate their familiarity with several basic agile practices. The nature of the following tasks will depend on the agile maturity level of the team as well as the organization. These tasks might range from a teaching assignment where the candidate lectures a team to a coaching exercise which provides feedback on a practice the team is already applying.

Note: If you are familiar with the Shu-Ha-Ri concept, you will most likely encounter tasks and exercises from the Shu or Ha parts.

The following are some exercises.

Create a Concept of a Dashboard or an Information Radiator

I can assume that it is now considered commonplace that transparency and visualizations are essential ingredients for any successful agile transition. If the team is not utilizing these elements, the scrum master should very well kick-off the effort. Start the exercise with collecting and aggregating suitable data, then derive information from it and, finally, visualize the acquired knowledge in a way that helps the team and the organization to grow.

In this dashboard exercise, you might be asked to create an initial version of such a team information radiator. Suitable team metrics that are readily available by questionnaires or polls are:

- The team happiness level,
- The team's trust level,
- The perceived value delivered to customers during the last sprint,
- The perceived current level of technical debt,
- The confidence level to meet a release date (especially if the organization is not shipping continuously), and

- The health level of the team or the organization:
  - The Scrum checklist of Henrik Kniberg works fine for this purpose
  - Alternatively, use the "The 'State of Agile' Checklist for Your Organization."
  - Determine whether team members would recommend working at the organization to a friend with an agile mindset. (This would be an employer Net Promoter Score [NPS] for the organization. **See also**: Wikipedia on the NPS.)

The information radiator can, of course, also provide quantitative performance data on the team, such as:

- Velocity, (**Note:** Be prepared to enter into a discussion on the usefulness of this metric, as well as the #NoEstimates discussion: why do we try to predict the future if the exercise has failed us over and over again?),
- The number of bugs,
- The lead-time and cycle-time.

Traditional metrics (such as the number of new users gained, user churn, engagement levels, or revenue) may be worth considering. Also, branching out into the product discovery field may make an excellent addition to the information radiator. Why not list your current hypotheses or experiments, and the date of your next user-test? The desired outcome of this exercise is not a functional dashboard but to start a discussion among team members and stakeholders. A concept for the dashboard provides, however, good insight into the candidate's agile mindset.

Read More: "Agile Metrics — The Good, the Bad, and the Ugly."

Note: Acquiring information from stakeholders might prove to be somewhat tricky. Just use the metrics that are available from the team or some software.

Create a Stakeholder Communication Concept

This part of the trial day assesses the future scrum master's communication capabilities. "Selling" the product and engineering organization to stakeholders (and the rest of the organization) is not only valuable but also an essential trait for furthering an agile transition or maintaining its momentum.

Winning hearts and minds will be critical in siloed legacy organizations that adhere to command and control structures outside of the product and engineering organization. Stakeholder communication is also crucial in fast-growing startups which exhibit a lack of organizational structure – and particularly those that are sales- or marketing-driven.

The task for the candidate will be to design a basic communication strategy for stakeholder communication that is suited to support transparency, interaction, and collaboration.

Read More: "10 Proven Stakeholder Communication Tactics during an Agile Transition."

POSSIBLE EXERCISES DURING A TRIAL DAY

Create a Definition of Ready (DoR)

The DoR defines a standard that product backlog items need to meet before the product owner can pick them to become items of the sprint backlog. The purpose of the DoR is simple: it ensures that the flow of the development team is not unnecessarily interrupted by a sloppy preparation at the user story or technical task level.

Typically, the DoR contains criteria such as:

1. An available description,
2. Defined acceptance criteria,
3. Deliverable by the team within a sprint,
4. All available deliverables (e.g., front-end designs),
5. Identified dependencies,
6. Defined performance criteria (if applicable),
7. Defined tracking criteria, and
8. The team's estimate.

Creating the DoR is usually a fifteen-minute team exercise that is well suited for time-boxing and silent writing of sticky-notes, which is followed by a brief discussion among the teammates. This exercise helps create a version 1.0 of the DoR, and the team can iterate on that over the next sprints.

Note: If you participate in a product backlog refinement and the DoR is missing, you may want to address this potential anti-pattern.

There is an interesting discussion in the agile community as to whether the DoR constitutes an anti-pattern in and by itself.

Mike Cohn points to the risk that the DoR can be considered as a kind of stage-gate approval process. (**Read More**: "The Dangers of a Definition of Ready.")

More often than not, dogmatism opens the door to misuse, and the DoR is no exception to this tenet. Nevertheless, I believe that the DoR is an excellent means to improve the user story creation process (in general). Particularly if used with common sense, it creates a shared understanding among all team members.

Create a Definition of Done (DoD)

The DoD defines a standard of what needs to be accomplished by the scrum team before a user story or a task can be labeled "potentially shippable."

In most cases, creating the DoD demands a higher effort than the DoR as it is often intertwined with more processes, or other functional entities, of the organization. For example, the DoD always extends into engineering practices, like continuous integration or continuous delivery. However, governance or legal issues might also be affected one way or another, depending on the kind of product or its maturity level.

The following list of criteria provides a good starting point for any discussion or exercise with the scrum team, leading to the creation of a DoD:

- A delivery standard as defined by the team,

- It contains all requirements to get a user story into production,
- The fitness for use is evident (enough value was built to justify releasing?),
- The external quality is verified (we have built the right thing?), and
- The internal quality is verified by unit tests are written – and all tests are green,
- The code is checked in,
- The code review was completed,
- All improvements from the code review were implemented,
- All existing unit tests remain green,
- The acceptance tests were verified by the development team,
- All integration tests were passed, and the
- Status of "done" was confirmed by the product owner.
- The following criteria are often overlooked and also need to be checked:
- Was the technical documentation updated?
- Was the user documentation updated?
- Was the user documentation localized?
- The localization for the task is done.
- The localization testing is done.
- The marketing input is done.
- The legal documents are done.

Again, iterating on the DoD is recommended: start small, then improve. (Inspecting and adapting as usual.)

Note: Large-Scale Scrum (LeSS) has a significantly broadened idea of a DoD. (**Read More:** "LeSS' idea regarding DoD.")

Participating in Scrum Ceremonies

There Are Plenty of Scrum Ceremonies

There are plenty of scrum ceremonies to choose from when it comes to a trial day for the scrum master candidate. The problem is, though, that except for the retrospective the majority of scrum ceremonies offers little room for a candidate to shine. On the one side, he or she lacks context as well as personal relationships with team members. On the other side, these ceremonies are usually driven by other team members than the scrum master. However, in this situation, the candidate can prove his or her knowledge and professionalism by observing and analyzing what is going with the unbiased mind of an outsider. This approach often leads to insights the scrum team member are not aware of.

The Retrospective: Using Classic Exercises for a Scrum Master Trial Day

Along with the product backlog refinement, the retrospective is by far the best-suited exercise for a trial day. An experienced scrum master can easily facilitate a retrospective for a new and unfamiliar team. With every scrum master having their way of handling a retrospective, chances are the team will be pushed out of its comfort zone. And if the team is willing to offer the benefit of the doubt, there might be more of a chance to identify previously unknown issues. Therefore, what exercise could be better suited to "inspect & adapt?"

Invest in Preparing for the Retrospective

By retrospective, I don't propose the basic, 30-minute version of "good, bad, and 2 actions items". I would suggest something more sophisticated as outlined in "Agile Retrospectives: Making Good Teams Great," a book by Esther Darby and Diana Larsen. Esther and Diana distinguish five stages of a retrospective:

1. Setting the stage,
2. Gathering data,
3. Generating insights,
4. Deciding what to do, and
5. Closing the retrospective.

I recommend that the candidate have a set of exercises ready. Sketching the activities in advance and bringing them to the trial day is even better.

Preparing for the Retrospective with Retromat

If you are not yet using Retromat by Corinna Baldauf, you should consider doing so. A lot of suitable exercises for retrospectives are aggregated in Retromat, covering all five stages. As a first step, I recommend going through all of these exercises and choosing from them for each category. Although the activities are supposed to be interchangeable, a random, unmindful combination of exercises may not work that well together. For instance, some combinations may break a cohesive story – and as the facilitator of a retrospective with an unfamiliar team, the candidate must own the narrative.

Once you have carefully identified all five exercises, a retrospective based on Retromat may look like this election manifesto for change.

Sprint Retrospective Anti-Patterns

What ceremony could better embody scrum's "inspect and adapt" mantra than the retrospective? I assume all agile peers agree that even the simplest retrospective – if only held regularly – is far more useful than having a fancy one once in a while, or in the worst case having none at all. No matter the frequency of your retrospectives, there is always room for improvement.

And in the unfortunate case that you only observe the retrospective and cannot run one, you may want to look out for anti-patterns. Learn more about the 21 common sprint retrospective anti-patterns that you should always watch out for.

Sprint Retrospective Anti-Patterns of the Scrum Team

- **#NoRetro**: There is no retrospective as the team believes there is nothing to improve. (There is no such thing as an agile nirvana where everything is just perfect. As people should say: becoming agile is a journey, not a destination, and there is always something to improve.)
- **Dispensable buffer:** The team cancels retrospectives if more time is needed to accomplish the sprint commitment/forecast. (The retrospective as a sprint emergency reserve is a typical sign of cargo cult agile. I believe that this exhibits a worse anti-pattern than not having a retrospective because there is presumably nothing to improve. That is just an all too human fallacy bordering on hubris. However, randomly canceling the retrospective to achieve a sprint goal is a clear sign that the team does not understand basic agile principles – such as continuous improvement. If the scrum team repeatedly does not meet a sprint goal, it should determine why. So, guess which scrum ceremony is designed for this purpose?)
- **Rushed retro**: The team is in a hurry and allocates much less than the usually necessary 60 to 90 minutes for a retrospective. (This is a slippery slope and it will probably end up as a ritualized ceremony of little value. Sooner or later, most team members will likely regard it as a waste of time. Do it right by allocating whatever time is needed. If the team considers not having retrospectives, why wouldn't they abandon scrum altogether?)
- **Someone sings**: Someone from the participants provides information on the retrospective to an outsider. (For

retrospectives, a Vegas Rule applies: what is said in the room, stays in the room. There is no exception to this rule.)

- **Extensive whining**: The team uses the retrospective primarily to complain about the situation, assuming the victim's role. (Change requires reflection, and occasionally it is a good exercise to let off steam. However, not moving on once you have identified critical issues and suggested changes, defies the purpose of the retrospective. Limiting the number of stickies to 2-3 per participant may help to change this attitude. You may also consider balancing positive and negative feedback by handing out an equal number of green and red stickies. In my opinion, this may appear to be a bit too rigid, though.)

- **UNSMART:** The team chooses to tackle UNSMART actions. (Bill Wake created the SMART acronym for reasonable action items: S – Specific, M – Measurable, A – Achievable, R – Relevant, T – Time-boxed. If the team picks UNSMART action items, though, it sets itself up for failure, contributing to a bias that agile is not working. This perception is random at best. **Read More**: "INVEST in Good Stories, and SMART Tasks.")

- **#NoAccountability:** Action items were accepted, however, no one was chosen to be responsible for delivery. (If the team is supposed to fix X, it is likely that everyone will rely on their other teammates to handle it. Appoint someone to be accountable, instead.)

- **Action what?** The team does not check the status of the action items from the previous retrospectives. (The sibling of autonomy is accountability. If the team is not following up on what they previously wanted to improve, it is curious as to why they picked action items in the first place. BILD Action items accounting)

Sprint Retrospective Anti-Patterns of the Development Team

Product owner non grata: The product owner is not welcome to the retrospective. Some purists still believe that only the development team and the scrum master shall attend the team's retrospective. However, the Scrum Guide refers to the scrum team as including the product owner. And it does so for a good reason: the team members either win together, or the team loses together. Of what benefit would it be to exclude the product owner?

Sprint Retrospective Anti-Patterns of the Scrum Master

- **Waste of time:** The team does not collectively value the retrospective. (If some team members consider the retrospective to be of little or no value, it is most often the retrospective itself that sucks. It may be time to re-evaluate. Is it the same procedure every time, ritualized and boring? Have a meta-retrospective on the retrospective itself. Change the venue. Have a beer- or wine-driven retrospective. There are so many things a scrum master can do to make retrospectives exciting and valuable again, reducing the absence rate. Furthermore, it is good to remember that (in my experience) introverts like to take part in retrospectives also.)
- **Prisoners:** Some team members only participate because they are forced to team up. (Don't pressure anyone to take part in a retrospective. Instead, make it worth their time. The drive to continuously improve as a team needs to be fueled by intrinsic motivation, neither by fear nor by order. **Tip**:

Retromat's "Why are you here?" exercise is a good opener for a retrospective from time to time.)

- **Groundhog day:** The retrospective never changes in composition, venue, or length. (In this case, the tendency is that the team will revisit the same issues over and over again – it's like groundhog day without the happy ending.)
- **Let's have it next sprint:** The team postpones the retrospective into the next sprint. (Beyond the "inspect & adapt" task, the retrospective serves as a moment of closure, helping reset everybody's mind so that the team can focus on the goal of the upcoming sprint. Postponing it into the upcoming sprint may also interrupt the flow of the team, and delay tackling possible improvements by up to a sprint. This is why it is important to have the retrospective before the planning of the follow-up sprint.)
- **#NoDocumentation**: No one is taking minutes for later use. (A retrospective is a substantial investment for many reasons and should be taken seriously. Taking notes and photos supports the process.)
- **No psychological safety**: The retrospective is an endless cycle of blame and finger-pointing. (The team wins together, the team loses together. Unfortunately, the blame game documents both the failure of the scrum master as the facilitator of the retrospective as well as the team's lack of maturity and communication skills.)
- **Bullying:** One or two team members are dominating the retrospective. (This communication behavior is often a sign of either a weak or uninterested scrum master. The retrospective needs to be a safe place where everyone–introverts included–can address issues and provide their feedback free from team members who are dominating the conversation, bullying or intimidating other

teammates. The failure to provide a safe place will result in participants dropping out of the retrospective and render the results obsolete. It is the main responsibility of the scrum master to ensure that everyone can be heard and has an opportunity to voice their thoughts. According to Google, equally distributed speaking time fosters and signifies a high-performing team. **Read More:** "What Google Learned From Its Quest to Build the Perfect Team.")

- **Stakeholder alert:** Stakeholders participate in the retrospective. (There are plenty of scrum ceremonies that address the communication needs of stakeholders: the sprint review, the product backlog refinement, the daily scrums – not to mention opportunities of having a conversation at water coolers, over coffee, or during lunchtime. If that spectrum of possibilities is still not sufficient, feel free to have additional meetings. However, the retrospective is off-limits to stakeholders.)

- **Passivity:** The team members are present but are not participating. (There are plenty of reasons for such behavior: they regard the retrospective a waste of time, it is an unsafe place, or the participants are bored to death by its predictiveness. The team members may also fear negative repercussions should they be absent, or maybe a homogenous group of introverts was unwittingly hired. Whatever the reason, there is likely no quick fix. The scrum master needs to determine what style of retrospective will work best in their organization's context.)

Sprint Retrospective Anti-Patterns of the Organization

- **No suitable venue:** There is no adequate place available to run the retrospective. (The least appropriate venue is a meeting room with a rectangular table surrounded by chairs. Sadly, it is the most common venue to convene a retrospective. Becoming agile requires a fresh and appropriate space. If this is not available, just be creative and go somewhere else. If the weather is beautiful, grab stickies and go outside. Or rent a suitable space anywhere else. If this is not possible, say, due to budget issues, remove at least the table so you can sit or stand in a circle. **Read More:** "Agile Workspace: The Undervalued Success Factor.")

- **Line managers present:** Line managers participate in retrospectives. (This is the worst anti-pattern I can think of. Like Bullying (above) it turns the retrospective into an unsafe place, thwarting an open discussion among the team members. Any line manager who insists on being included shows their lack of understanding of basic agile practices. **Hint**: If you are a small product delivery team at a start-up and your part-time scrum master (or product owner) also serves in a management function, retrospectives could be challenging. In this case, consider hiring an external scrum master to facilitate meaningful retrospectives.)

- **Let us see your minutes**: Someone from the organization (outside the team) requests access to the retrospective minutes. (This is almost as bad as line managers who want to participate in a retrospective. Of course, the access must be denied.)

Conclusion

With many ways in which a retrospective can be a failure (even if it looks favorable at first glance), I would suggest that these are the three most important retrospective anti-patterns : (1) not making the retrospective a safe place, (2) unequally distributed speaking time, and (3) a ritualized format that never changes.

The Daily Scrum or Stand-up

Including the stand-up as part of the trial day is a no-brainer, and also a smart stratagem. A good team needs five to ten minutes for a stand-up, thereby limiting the candidate's ability to observe possible anti-patterns. However, given that the stand-up is the scrum ceremony with the highest potential for anti-pattern density, it is an effective means to test the candidate.

The following are some typical stand-up anti-patterns:

- **No routine:** The stand-up does not happen at the same time and the same place every day. (While routine has the potential to ruin every retrospective, it is helpful in the context of stand-ups. Think of it as a spontaneous drill: don't put too much thought into the stand-up, just do it. Skipping stand-ups can turn out to be a slippery slope. And skipping may only be accepted the day after the sprint planning. However, please keep in mind that every team member can veto skipping the stand-up.)
- **Status report:** The stand-up is a status report meeting: team members wait in line to report specific progress to the scrum master, the product owner, and maybe even a stakeholder.
- **Ticket numbers only:** Updates often sound generic, with little or no value to others. (For example:"Yesterday, I worked on X-123. Today, I will work on X-129.")

- **Problem-solving:** Discussions are triggered to solve problems (instead of parking the issues so they can be addressed after the stand-up).
- **Planning meeting:** The team hijacks the stand-up to discuss new requirements, refine user stories, or hold a sort of (sprint) planning meeting.
- **No red dots:** No team member offers help to a member who has experienced difficulties in accomplishing an issue over several consecutive days. (This signifies that they either do not trust each other, do not care for each other, or the utilization of the team is maximized.)
- **Monologs:** Team members violate their (60 to 90 seconds) time-boxing, and start monologues.
- **Statler and Waldorf:** A few team members comment on every issue (which is a waste of time and annoyingly patronizing).
- **Disrespect I:** Some team members show disrespect by talking while someone is sharing their progress with the team. (The need to use speak tokens among adult team members is similarly irritating.)
- **Assignments:** Either the product owner or the scrum master assigns tasks directly to team members.
- **Cluelessness:** Team members show they are not prepared for the stand-up. (For example: "I was doing some stuff, but I cannot remember what — was important, though.")
- **Let's start the shift:** The stand-up functions like an artificial factory siren signifying the start of the next work shift. (This is a common Taylorism artifact showing that trust in the team is missing.)
- **Disrespect II:** Team members arrive late to the stand-up.

(**Note**: If the time for the stand-up was not chosen by the team it could indicate distrust by the management.)

- **Excessive feedback:** Team members tend to quickly criticize other members, sparking a discussion within the stand-up rather than outside its confines.
- **Overcrowded:** Stand-ups are ineffective due to a large number of active participants.
- **Talkative chickens:** "Chickens" actively participate in the stand-up. (However, even though they are expected to listen in merely, I believe it is acceptable if a stakeholder asks a question during a stand-up.)
- **Anti-agile:** Line managers that attend stand-ups only to gather "performance data" on individual team members. (This behavior defies the very purpose of self-organizing teams.)

Depending on the context, it may also be an anti-pattern if the product owner or a stakeholder is introducing new tickets to the current sprint during the stand-up.

Be aware that another issue (potentially uncovered during the stand-up) is an offline board that has room for improvement. Some candidates may prefer a direct approach, and point out any controversial issues with it. Personally, I believe that the scrum team should build its offline board, and not the scrum master, so I would instead ask questions that point the team in the right direction.

Some teams like to have stand-ups in Slack, particularly those that are not co-located. If that is the case, make sure that you can pair with someone to effectively follow it.

Lastly, if the working space is tight, you can forestall the

PARTICIPATING IN SCRUM CEREMONIES

rudeness of people who walk by a team in front of a board during the stand-up. Be proactive and speak up to address this behavior. (No joke, this was an actual situation in a previous project of mine.)

Read More: "16 Stand-up Anti-Patterns Threatening Your Transition to Scrum."

The Product Backlog Refinement

From a candidate's perspective, it is best to participate in a product backlog refinement session, helping the team to improve the PO's product backlog. The idiom is essential here: garbage in, garbage out.

PRODUCT BACKLOG REFINEMENT PROCESS

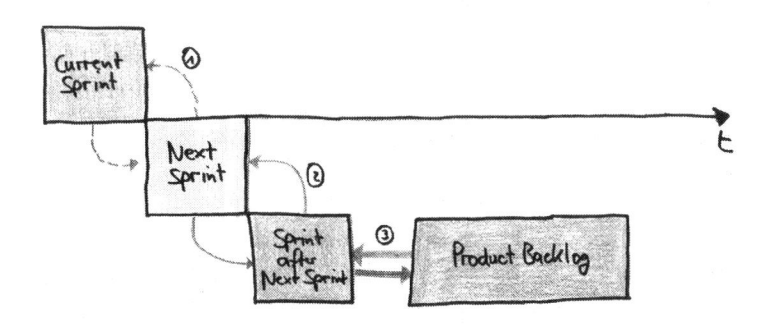

© STEFAN WOLPERS, 2016

A product backlog refinement session provides you with the opportunity to demonstrate beneficial practices by addressing:

- How to deal with large product backlogs,
- What the ideal size of a product backlog is,
- How to apply Bill Wake's INVEST principle to create user stories,
- How to slice user-stories based on end-to-end functions (and not on components),
- How to manage acceptance criteria (for example, recommending the use of Gherkin for…),
- How to demystify DoR (definition of ready),
- The whole estimation process vs. an alternative estimates process (like estimation poker, knowledge transfer, #NoEstimates, predictability as an agile key metric), and
- How to defuse the original sprint planning ceremony with regular product backlog refinement sessions.

A good candidate will ask the right questions during the refinement session without having detailed knowledge about the product backlog itself. Handling the process and its principles are the specific focus of this exercise. Observing the team during the product backlog refinement will reveal existing anti-patterns and provide plenty of opportunities to start a discussion with the team. I have identified the following five refinement anti-pattern categories:

General Product Backlog Anti-Patterns

- **Prioritization by proxy:** A single stakeholder or a committee of stakeholders prioritize the product backlog. (The strength of scrum is building on the strong position of the product owner. The product owner is the only person to decide what tasks become product backlog items. Hence, the product owner also decides on the priority. Take away that empowerment, and scrum turns into a pretty robust waterfall 2.0 process.)
- **100% in advance:** The scrum team creates a product backlog upfront, covering the complete project or product because the scope of the release is limited. (Question: how can you be sure to know now what to deliver in six months?)
- **Over-sized:** The product backlog contains more items than the scrum team can ship within three to four sprints. (By doing this, the product owner is creating waste by hoarding issues that might never materialize.)
- **Outdated issues:** The product backlog contains items that haven't been touched for six to eight weeks or more. (Typically, this is the length of time for two to four sprints. If the product owner is hoarding backlog items, older items may become outdated, and render previously invested work by the scrum team obsolete.)
- **Everything is estimated:** All user stories of the product backlog are detailed and estimated. (Too much upfront work bears the risk of misallocating the scrum team's time.)
- **Component-based items:** The product backlog items are sliced horizontally, based on components, instead of vertically, based on end-to-end features. (This may be caused by your organizational structure – or maybe the team

and product owner need a workshop on writing user stories? Moving to cross-functional teams will improve the team's ability to deliver.)

- **Missing acceptance criteria:** There are user stories in the product backlog without acceptance criteria. (It is not necessary to have acceptance criteria at the beginning the refinement cycle, although this would make the task much easier. In the end, however, all user stories need to meet the DoR standard, and acceptance criteria are a part of that definition.)

- **No more than a title:** The product backlog contains user stories with nothing more than a title (see above).

- **Issues too detailed:** There are user stories with an extensive list of acceptance criteria. (Typically, three to five acceptance criteria are more than sufficient, but it is considered extreme when the product owner covers each edge case without negotiating with the team.)

- **Neither themes nor epics:** The product backlog is not structured by themes or epics. (This is a problem that makes it hard to align individual items with the "big picture" of the organization. The product backlog should not be an assortment of isolated tasks, or a massive to-do-list.)

- **No research:** The product backlog contains few to no spikes. (This often correlates with a team that is spending too much time on discussing prospective problems, instead of researching them with a spike as a part of an iterative user story creation process.)

Product Backlog Anti-Patterns at Portfolio and Product Roadmap Level

- **Roadmap?** The product backlog is not reflecting the roadmap. (The product backlog is supposed to be granular only for the first two or three sprints. Beyond that point, the product backlog should rather focus on themes and epics from the product roadmap. If those are not available, the product backlog is likely too granular.)

- **Annual roadmaps:** The organization's portfolio plan, as well as the release plan or product roadmap, are created once a year in advance. (If the product backlog stays aligned to this practice, it introduces waterfall planning through the back door. Agile planning is always continuous; at the portfolio level, the plan needs to be revised at least every three months.)

- **Roadmaps kept secret:** The portfolio planning and the release plan or product roadmap are not visible to everybody. (As L. Carroll expressed: "If you do not know where you are going, any road will get you there." This planning information is crucial for any scrum team and needs to be highly visible and available to everybody at any time.)

- **China in your hands:** The portfolio planning and the release plan or the product roadmap are not considered achievable and believable. (If this is reflected in the product backlog, then working on user stories will probably be a waste of time.)

Product Backlog Anti-Patterns of the Product Owner

- **Storage for ideas:** The product owner uses the product backlog as a repository of ideas and requirements. (This practice clogs the product backlog. It may lead to a cognitive

overload, and makes alignment with the big picture at portfolio management and roadmap planning level very tough.)
- **Part-time PO:** The product owner does not work daily on the product backlog. (At any given time, the product backlog needs to represent the best use of the development team's resources. Updating it once a week before the next refinement session does not suffice to meet this requirement.)
- **Copy & paste PO:** The product owner creates user stories by breaking down requirement documents received from stakeholders into smaller chunks. (This scenario helped to coin the nickname "ticket monkey" for the product owner, reminding us that user story creation is a team exercise.)
- **Dominant PO:** The product owner creates user stories by providing not just the "why", but also the "how" and the "what". (The team answers the how question with the technical implementation and both the team and the PO collaborate on the what question by determining the scope that is necessary to achieve the desired purpose.)
- **INVEST?** The product owner apparently does not apply the INVEST principle by Bill Wake to user stories.
- **Issues too detailed:** The product owner invests too much time upfront in user stories, making the stories too explicit. (If a user story looks complete, the team members might not see the necessity to get involved in a further refinement. This way a "fat" user story reduces the engagement level of the team, compromising the creation of a shared understanding. Curiously, this did not happen back when we used index cards, maybe given their physical limitation.)
- **What team?** The product owner does not involve the entire scrum team in the refinement process but, rather, just a

"lead engineer"— or any other member of the team independently of the others. (There is no lead engineer in a scrum team.)

- **"Know it all" PO:** The product owner does not involve stakeholders or subject matter experts in the refinement process. (A product owner with this principle is perceived as omniscient or a communication gateway, and is a risk to the scrum team's success.)

Product Backlog Anti-Patterns of the Development Team

- **Submissive team:** The development team submissively follows the demands of the product owner. (It is the meritorious obligation of every team member to challenge the product owner as to whether or not the selection of issues is the best use of the development team's time.)
- **What technical debt?** The development team does not demand adequate resources for tackling technical debt and bugs. (The rule of thumb is that 25% of resources are allocated in every sprint for fixings bugs and refactoring the code base.)
- **No slack-time:** The development team does not demand 20% slack time from the product owner. (This anti-pattern cannot be addressed early enough – and it overlaps with sprint planning and the team's commitment. If a team's capacity is always utilized at 100%, its performance will decrease over time: Everyone will focus on getting tasks done. There will be less time to support teammates or to pair. Small issues will no longer be immediately addressed. Ultimately, the member attitude of "I am too busy" will

demoralize the team and make them question why they do what they do.)

Relative Team Capacity and Allocation for Sprint Planning

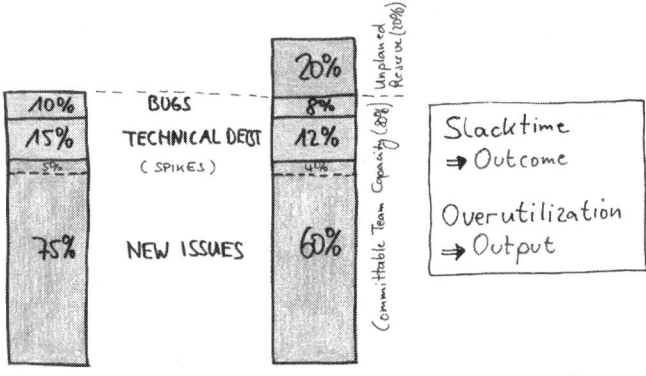

10%	BUGS	20%
15%	TECHNICAL DEBT (SPIKES)	8%
		12%
		4%
75%	NEW ISSUES	60%

Unplanned Reserve (20%)
Committable Team Capacity (80%)

Slacktime ⇒ Outcome
Overutilization ⇒ Output

© Stefan Wolpers, 2017. (Age-of-Product.com)

Product Backlog Anti-Patterns of the Scrum Team

- **No time for refinement:** The team does not have enough refinement sessions, resulting in a low-quality backlog. (The Scrum Guide advises spending up to 10% of the scrum team's time on the product backlog refinement. This is a sound business decision: nothing is more expensive than a feature that is not delivering any value.)
- **Too much refinement:** The team has too many refinement

sessions, resulting in an over-detailed backlog. (Too much refinement can be unhealthy also.)

- **No DoR:** The scrum team has not created a DoR which the product backlog items need to match before becoming selectable for a sprint. (A simple checklist like the DoR can significantly improve the scrum team's work. It will increase the quality of the resulting user stories, as well as the general way of working as a team.)

Read More: "Product Backlog Refinement — Agile Transition (Part 2)."

The Sprint Planning

The purpose of the sprint planning is to align both the development team and the product owner on what potentially shippable product increment shall be delivered in the upcoming sprint.

The development team's commitment should hence reflect the product owner's sprint goal. Also, the team needs to come up with a plan on how to accomplish its commitment.

Personally, the sprint planning (which originally comprises parts I and II) is a less well-suited exercise for the trial day. Here are two main reasons for this opinion:

- If the scrum team has been heretofore successfully using product backlog refinements, the candidate's part in the sprint planning I would be limited. There would be no more to do than witness how the development team and the product owner adjust the previously discussed scope (of the upcoming sprint) to the available capacity. If someone from the development team is unexpectedly not available on the next sprint, one or two tasks would have to go back to the product backlog. Or, if a highly valuable new task appeared overnight, and the product owner wanted this task to become a part of the next sprint backlog, some other user story would need to go back to the product backlog. A good team would be able to handle this in five to ten minutes before moving on to sprint planning II.

- The candidate also could not actively participate in the development team's sprint planning II, when the team breaks down the first set of sprint backlog items into subtasks. (The sprint planning II often takes one to three hours, during which there would be little or no communication between the development team and the candidate – which defies the purpose of the trial day.)

The only situation, which turns the sprint planning I into a valid exercise for the trial day, is a team that already has trouble facilitating a useful product backlog refinement. In this case, a lot of the ineffective practices would spill over into the sprint planning. These anti-patterns are the ones better suited for our purpose, which would be to have a meaningful trial day by addressing observed issues with the prospective teammates.

The following are three sets of common anti-patterns of the sprint planning.

Sprint Planning Anti-Patterns of the Development Team:

- **Any absentees?** The team members do not determine their availability at the beginning of the sprint planning. (Committing, in this situation, would be unlikely.)
- **Capacity?** The development team overestimates its capacity and takes on too many tasks. (Instead, the development team should take everything into account that might affect its ability to deliver. The list of those issues is long: public holidays, new team members, those on vacation leave, team members quitting, team members on sick leave, corporate overhead, scrum ceremonies, and other meetings (just to name a few.)
- **Ignoring technical debt:** The development team does not demand adequate capacity to tackle technical debt and bugs during the sprint. (The rule of thumb is that 25% of resources are allocated every sprint to fix bugs and refactor the code base. If the product owner ignores this accepted practice, and the development team allows this violation, the scrum team will find itself in a downward spiral concerning its future product delivery capabilities.)
- **No slack time:** The development team does not demand 20% slack time from the product owner. (If a team's capacity is always over-utilized, its performance will decrease over time, particularly in an organization with a volatile daily business. Everyone will focus on getting their tasks done. There will be less time to support teammates or to pair. The team will no longer promptly address smaller or urgent issues. Individual team members will become bottlenecks, which might seriously impede the flow within the team. The member attitude of "I am too busy" will demoralize the team, and overutilization will always push the individual team member to focus on their output. Preferentially, slack time will allow the scrum team to act collaboratively and focus on the outcome.)

- **Planning too detailed:** During sprint planning II, the development team plans every single subtask of the upcoming sprint. (Don't become too granular. Two-thirds of the subtasks would be more than sufficient, the rest will follow naturally during the sprint. Doing too much planning upfront may result in waste.)
- **Too much estimating:** The development team estimates subtasks. (Personally, this is accounting for the sake of accounting. Don't waste your time on this.)
- **Too little planning:** The development team skips the sprint planning II altogether. (Skipping the sprint planning II is unfortunate, as this time is also a good situation to discuss how to share knowledge with the development team. For example, the team should plan for who will be pairing with whom on what task. The sprint planning II is also well-suited for considering how to reduce technical debt.)
- **Team leads?** The development team does not collaboratively devise a plan to deliver on its commitment, rather, the "team lead" assigns tasks to individual team members. (There is a consensus that senior developers do not like the idea of no "team lead" in a scrum team. **Read More**: "Why Engineers Despise Agile.")

Sprint Planning Anti-Patterns of the Product Owner:

- **What are we fighting for?** The product owner finds it difficult to provide a sprint goal, or the chosen sprint goal is flawed. (An original sprint goal will answer the "What are we fighting for?" question, and is a negotiation between the product owner and the development team. It must be focused and measurable, as sprint goal and team

PARTICIPATING IN SCRUM CEREMONIES

commitment go hand in hand. Moreover, the sprint goal is a useful calibration for the upcoming sprint.)

- **Calling Kanban 'Scrum':** The sprint backlog resembles a random assortment of tasks, and there is no defined sprint goal. (If this is the normal way of finishing your sprint planning I, you have probably outlived the usefulness of scrum as a product development framework. Depending on the maturity of your product, Kanban may prove to be a better solution in this case. Otherwise, the randomness may signal a weak product owner who may listen too much to stakeholders instead of appropriately prioritizing the product backlog.)

- **Unfinished business:** Unfinished user stories and other tasks from the last sprint have spilled over into the upcoming sprint without any discussion. (There might be good reasons for this, and one example may be that the tasks' value has not changed. Considering the sunk cost fallacy, it should never be an automatism, though.)

- **Last minute changes:** The product owner tries to squeeze in some last-minute user stories that do not meet the DoR. (Principally, it is the prerogative of the product owner to make such changes, to ensure that the development team is working only on the most valuable user stories at any given time. However, if the scrum team is regularly practicing product backlog refinement sessions, these occurrences should be rare. If they happen frequently, it indicates that the product owner needs help with prioritization and team communication. Or, the product owner may need support to say "no" more often to stakeholders.)

- **Output focus:** The product owner pushes the development team to take on more tasks than it can realistically handle. Likely, the product owner is referring to former team metrics, such as velocity, to support their desire. (This would be an opportunity for the candidate to step in and address the issue.)

Sprint Planning Anti-Patterns of the Scrum Team:

- **Irregular sprint lengths:** The scrum team has variable sprint cadences, and tasks are not sized to fit into the regular sprint length. Instead, the sprint length has been adapted to the size of the tasks. (While it is quite common to extend the sprint length at the end of the year when most of the team members are on holiday, there is no reason to deviate from the regular cadence during the rest of the year. Rather than changing the sprint length, the scrum team should invest more effort into sizing epics and user stories in the correct way.)
- **Over-commitment:** The scrum team regularly takes on too many tasks and simply moves unfinished work to the next sprint. (It may be common for two or three items to spill over to the next sprint, but if 30-40 percent of the original commitment is regularly not delivered during the sprint, the scrum team may have created a sort of "time-boxed Kanban." This could be the right time to ask the team whether moving to Kanban might be a helpful alternative.)
- **Stage-gate by DoR:** The DoR is handled dogmatically and creates a stage-gate type of approval process. (This is an interesting topic for a discussion among scrum team members: should a valuable user story be postponed to another sprint just because the front end designs will not be available for another two working days? Take the discussion to the team. If the members agree with the circumstances and accept the user story into the sprint, then that is fine.
Read More: "The Dangers of a Definition of Ready."

- **Ignoring the DoR:** The development team does not reject user stories that do not meet the DoR. (This is the opposite of being dogmatic about the application of DoR: not ready user stories will cause unnecessary disruptions during the sprint if they are allowed into it. Laissez-faire will also cause problems.)

- **Forecast imposed:** The sprint commitment is not a team-based decision or free of outside influence. (There are several anti-patterns to consider: an assertive product owner dominates the development team by defining in advance the scope of the commitment, a stakeholder points at the team's previous velocity and demands taking on more user stories [to presumably fill free capacity], or the "tech lead" of the development team is making a commitment on behalf of the team. Whatever the reason, the candidate should address the underlying issue[s].)

- **Planning ignored:** The development team does not collectively participate in the sprint planning but is represented by one or two team members – possibly the tech and UX leads. (There should never be one or two "leading" teammates in a scrum team [see above]. And unless you are using LeSS [no pun intended], where teams are only represented in the overall sprint planning, the whole scrum team needs to participate. Because it is a team effort, everyone's voice needs to be heard.)

The Sprint Anti-Patterns

The sprint is neither an official scrum ceremony nor an artifact. Apparently, it is not a role either. It is merely a timebox. Still, there are plenty of sprint anti-patterns to make your life as a scrum team more difficult than necessary.

If there is only one trial day available, the candidate will hardly have time to notice (the following list of) sprint anti-patterns. These usually reveal themselves to the observer over time. Recognizing the sprint anti-patterns often requires social interaction beyond attending scrum ceremonies, also. Even so, I recommend keeping them in mind.

This list of notorious sprint anti-patterns applies to the development team, the product owner, the scrum master, the scrum team and also the stakeholders.

Sprint Anti-Patterns of the Product Owner

- **Absent PO:** The product owner is missing most of the sprint and therefore not available to answer questions from the development team. (This creates a micro-waterfall approach for the duration of the sprint.)
- **Tenacious PO:** The product owner cannot let go of product backlog items once they become sprint backlog items. For example, the product owner increases the scope of a user story, or they change acceptance criteria once the team has accepted the issue into the sprint backlog. (There is a definite line here: before a product backlog item turns into a sprint backlog item, the product owner is responsible. However, once it moves from one backlog to the other, the development team becomes responsible. If changes become acute during the sprint, the team will collaboratively decide on how to handle them.)
- **Inflexible PO:** The product owner is not flexible enough to adjust acceptance criteria. (If the work on a task reveals that

the agreed upon acceptance criteria are no longer achievable or it is waste, the scrum team needs to adapt to the new reality. Blindly following the original plan violates a core scrum principle.)

- **Delaying PO:** The product owner does not accept sprint backlog items once they are finished. Instead, the PO waits until the end of the sprint. (In the spirit of continuous integration, the product owner should immediately check tasks that meet the acceptance criteria. Otherwise, the product owner will create an artificial queue which will increase the cycle time. This habit also puts reaching the sprint goal at risk.)

- **Misuse of sprint cancellation:** The product owner cancels sprints to impose their will upon the team. (It is the prerogative of the product owner to cancel sprints. However, the product owner should not do this without a serious cause. The product owner should also never abort a sprint without consulting the development team first. Most likely, the team has an idea how to save the sprint. Lastly, misusing the cancellation privilege could also indicate a team collaboration issue.)

- **No sprint cancellation:** The product owner does not cancel a sprint when the sprint goal can no longer be achieved. (For example, if the product owner identified a unifying sprint goal, like integrating a new payment method, and the management then abandons that payment method mid-sprint, continuing to work on the sprint goal would be waste. In a futile case such as this, the product owner should cancel the sprint.)

Sprint Anti-Patterns of the Development Team

- **No WIP limit:** There is no work in progress limit for the team. (The purpose of the sprint is to deliver a potentially shippable product increment that provides value to either the customers or the organization. This goal requires getting something done by the end of the sprint. The flow theory suggests that the productivity of a team improves with a WIP limit. This limit defines the largest number of tasks a team can work on at the same time. Exceeding the WIP number results in creating extra queues which reduce the throughput of the team. The cycle time, which is the period between starting and finishing a ticket, measures this effect.)
- **Cherry-picking:** The team cherry-picks its work. (This anti-pattern often overlays with the above WIP issue. Human beings are motivated by short-term gratification. It just feels good to solve yet another puzzle from the board — like coding a new task. Contrary to this dopamine fix, checking how someone else solved another problem during code review would be less rewarding. Hence you often notice tickets queueing in the code review column, for example.)
- **Outdated board:** The team does not consistently update tickets on the board in time to reflect the current status. (The board, no matter if it is a physical or digital board, is vital for coordinating a team's work. It is also an integral part of the communication of the scrum team with its stakeholders. A board that is not up to date will impact the trust the stakeholders have on the scrum team. Deteriorating trust may then cause countermeasures on the side of the stakeholders. The [management] pendulum may swing back toward traditional methods as a consequence. The road back to PRINCE2 is paved with abandoned boards.)
- **Side gigs:** The team is working on issues that are not visible on the board. (While sloppiness is excusable, siphoning off resources and bypassing the product owner (who is

accountable for the scrum team's return on investment) is unacceptable. This behavior also signals a massive conflict within the "team." Given this display of distrust (Why wouldn't the engineers address this seemingly important issue before or during the sprint?) the team is functioning more as a group anyway.)

- **Gold plating:** The team increases the scope of sprints by adding unnecessary work to sprint backlog items. (This effect is also referred to as scope-stretching. The development team ignores the original scope agreement with the product owner. For whatever reason, the team enlarges the task without prior consultation with the product owner. This ignorance may result in a questionable allocation of resources. However, there is a simple solution: the developers and the product owner need to talk more often with each other. If the product owner is not yet co-located with the development team, now would be a right moment to reconsider.)

Sprint Anti-Patterns of the Scrum Master

- **Flow disruption:** The scrum master allows stakeholders to disrupt the workflow of the development team during the sprint. (There are several possibilities on how stakeholders can interrupt the flow of the team during a sprint. Any of the behaviors below will impede the team's productivity. The scrum master should prevent them from manifesting themselves:
    - The scrum master has a laissez-faire policy regarding access to the development team.
    - The scrum master does not object when management

invites engineers to random meetings as subject matter experts.
  - Lastly, the scrum master allows either the stakeholders or managers to turn the daily scrum into a reporting session.)

- **Lack of support:** The scrum master does not support team members who need help with a task. (Development teams often create tasks an engineer can finish within a day. However, if someone struggles with a task for more than two days without voicing that they need support, the scrum master should address the issue. Importantly, this is also the reason for marking tasks on a physical board with red dots each day if they haven't been moved on to the next column.)

- **Micromanagement:** The scrum master does not prevent the product owner — or anyone else — from assigning tasks to the engineers. (The development team organizes typically itself without external intervention. And the scrum master should act as the shield of the team in this respect.)

- **#NoRetro:** The scrum master does not gather data during the sprint that would support the team in the upcoming retrospective. (This is self-explanatory.)

Note: I do believe that it is not the task of the scrum master to move tickets on a whiteboard. The team members should do this during the stand-up. It is also not the responsibility of the scrum master to consistently update an online board so that it reflects the status of a corresponding physical board. Lastly, if the team considers a burndown chart helpful, the team members should be responsible for updating this after the stand-up. #justsaying

Sprint Anti-Patterns of the Scrum Team

- **A maverick & the sprint backlog:** Someone adds an item to the sprint backlog without first consulting the team. (The fixed scope of a sprint backlog — in the sense of workload — is at the core of enabling the team to make a commitment or forecast. Hence, the scope per se is untouchable during the sprint. Changes in the composition of a sprint backlog are possible, for example, when a critical bug pops up after a sprint's start. However, adding an issue such as this to the sprint backlog requires compensation. Another task of a similar size would need to go back to the product backlog. What all of these exceptions have in common is that the scrum team must collectively decide on them. No single teammate can add to or remove an item from the sprint backlog.)

- **Hardening sprint:** The scrum team decides to have a hardening or "clean up" sprint. (This one is simple: there is no such thing as a hardening sprint in Scrum. The goal of the sprint is to deliver a valuable and potentially shippable product increment. Most often, scrum teams agree in advance on a standard of what "done" means – also known as DoD or definition of done. Declaring buggy tasks as done thus violates core principles of the team's way of collaboration. A so-called hardening sprint is commonly a sign of a low-grade adoption of agile principles by the team or organization. This problem is likely when the team is not yet cross-functional. Or when quality assurance is still handled by a functional, non-agile silo with the product delivery organization.)

- **Delivering Y instead of X:** The product owner believes in building X. The development team is working on Y. (This is not merely a result of an inferior product backlog refinement. This anti-pattern indicates that the team failed to create a shared understanding. There are plenty of reasons for this to happen:

- The product owner and the development team members are not talking enough during the sprint. [The product owner may be too busy to answer questions from the team or attend the daily scrum. Or, the team may not be co-located.]
- No development team member has ever participated in user tests. Therefore, there is a lack of understanding among the engineers of the users' problems. [This is the reason why engineers should regularly interview users.]
- The product owner presented a user story that seemed ready but was too granular, and no one from the development team was concerned about thoroughly checking it. [If a granular user story is totally missing acceptance criteria, or the existing acceptance criteria missed the problem, then the team should always address the issue during the next retrospective.])

- **No sense of urgency:** There is no potentially shippable product increment at the end of a sprint. There was no reason given to cancel a sprint. It was deemed just an ordinary sprint. (These are signs that the scrum team lacks the sense of urgency to deliver at the end of a sprint. If it is acceptable to fail on delivering value at the end of a sprint, the whole idea behind scrum is questioned. Remember, a scrum team trades a commitment or forecast for inclusion in decision-making, autonomy, and self-organization. Creating a low-grade timeboxed Kanban and calling it "scrum" will not honor this deal. Therefore, it is in the best interest of the scrum team to endeavor to make each sprint's outcome releasable, even if it is not released.)

- **New kid on the block:** The scrum team welcomed a new team member during the sprint, forgetting to address the issue during sprint planning, and ended up overcommitted. (While it is acceptable to welcome new teammates during a sprint, the team needs to adjust its capacity during the sprint planning to account for the onboarding effort. The new team member should not be a surprise. However, it is an organizational anti-pattern if the newbie is a surprise.)

- **Variable sprint length:** The scrum team extends the sprint length by a few days to meet the sprint goal. (This is just another way of cooking the agile books to match a goal or a metric. This is not agile; it is just inconsequential. It is best to be honest and address the underlying issues as to why the team outcome does not meet the sprint goal. **Note**: I would not consider it an anti-pattern to deviate from a sprint length during a holiday season.)

Sprint Anti-Patterns of the IT management

- **All hands on deck without Scrum:** The management temporarily abandons scrum in an all hands on the pump situation. (This is a classic manifestation of disbelief in agile practices, fed by command and control thinking. Most likely, canceling sprints and gathering the scrum teams would also solve the issue at hand.)

- **Reassigning team members:** The management regularly assigns team members of one scrum team to another team. (Scrum can only live up to its potential if the team members can build trust with each other. The longevity of teams is essential. Moving people between teams, on the contrary, reflects a project-minded idea of management. It also ignores the preferred team building practice which scrum teams should discover for themselves. All members need to be on a team voluntarily. Scrum rarely works if team members are pressed into service. **Note**: It is not an anti-pattern, though, if two teams decide to exchange teammates temporarily. This exchange is an established practice for specialists to spread knowledge or mentor other colleagues.)

- **Special forces:** A manager assigns tasks directly to engineers, thus bypassing the product owner. (This behavior violates core scrum principles. It also indicates that the manager cannot let go of command and control practices. They continue to micromanage subordinates even though a scrum team could accomplish the task in a self-organized manner. This behavior demonstrates a level of ignorance that may require higher management support to deal with it.)

Sprint Anti-Patterns of Stakeholders

- **Pitching developers:** The stakeholders try to sneak in small tasks for the scrum team by pitching them directly to developers. (Nice Try #1.)
- **Everything is a bug:** The stakeholders try to speed up delivery from the scrum team by relabeling their tasks as serious bugs. (Nice Try #2. A particular case is placed in an "express lane" for bug fixes and other urgent issues. Every stakeholder usually tries to make their tasks eligible for that express lane.)

- **Disrupting the flow:** The stakeholders disrupt the flow of the scrum team. (See above, scrum master section.)

Conclusion

Although the sprint itself is just a timebox, there are plenty of sprint anti-patterns to observe. A lot of them are easy to fix by the scrum team. Other sprint anti-patterns, however, point at organizational issues that probably will require more than a retrospective to correct. Nevertheless, the candidate can provide valuable input for such a retrospective based on his or her unbiased observations.

The Sprint Review Anti-Patterns

From my perspective, the sprint review is the least suitable ceremony for a scrum master trial day.

The sprint review is all about the development team, the product owner, and the stakeholders determining whether they are on track delivering value to customers, as well as the organization (also known as 'inspect & adapt'). It is the best moment to create or reaffirm the shared understanding among all participants (by providing constructive feedback) as to whether the product backlog is still reflecting the best use of the scrum team's resources.

The sprint review is, therefore, an excellent opportunity to talk about the general progress of the product. All of this requires a substantial knowledge of the product – its future and its past, as well as the established relationships with everybody involved in the endeavor. None of this pertinent information would be available for the candidate to bring to the table at this point. Additionally, there is not much for a scrum master to do during the sprint review except to watch for anti-patterns or seek a discussion with stakeholders that attend the sprint review. (The latter is, though, indeed an interesting experience for gathering background information on how the scrum team is doing in general.)

The candidate might observe the following sprint review anti-patterns.

Sprint Review Anti-Patterns of the Product Owner

- **Selfish PO:** The product owner presents the team's accomplishments as though it was their own to the stakeholders. (This is unethical. Remember the old saying: "There is no 'I' in 'team'?")
- **Delayed sprint acceptance:** The product owner uses the sprint review information to accept user stories. (This should be decoupled from the sprint review. The product owner should accept user stories the moment they meet the acceptance criteria.)
- **Unapproachable PO**: The product owner is not accepting feedback from the stakeholders. (This behavior violates the prime purpose of the sprint review ceremony.)

Sprint Review Anti-Patterns of the Development Team

- **Death by PowerPoint:** Participants are usually bored to death by PowerPoint. (The foundation of a successful sprint review is "show, don't tell." Even better is to let the stakeholders drive the ceremony.)
- **Same faces again:** The same representatives from the development team always participate. (Unless the organization works with several teams based on LeSS (large-scale Scrum), this is not a good sign. The challenge, though, is that you cannot enforce the team's participation either. So, make it interesting enough that everyone wants to participate. **Note:** If the team does not religiously attend each sprint review at full strength, it is not an anti-pattern per se. However, there should be some rotation among participating team members.)
- **Side gigs:** The development team has been working on issues outside the sprint scope, and the product owner learns about those tasks for the first time during the sprint review.
- **Cheating:** The development team demos items that are still buggy. (There is a good reason to show unfinished work sometimes. But, buggy work violates the DoD at an unacceptable level.)

Sprint Review Anti-Patterns of the Scrum Team

- **Following a plan:** The scrum team does not use the sprint review to discuss the current state of the product or project with the stakeholders. (Again, getting feedback is the purpose of the exercise. A we-know-what-to-build attitude is bordering on hubris. **Read More**: "Sprint Review, a Feedback Gathering Event: 17 Questions and 8 Techniques.")

- **Sprint accounting:** There is a demo of every task accomplished, and stakeholders do not enthusiastically receive it. (Tell a compelling story at the beginning of the review to engage the stakeholders. Leave out those user stories that are not relevant to the story. Do not bore stakeholders by including everything that was accomplished. We are not accountants.)

Sprint Review Anti-Patterns of the Stakeholders

- **Scrum à la phase-gate:** The sprint review is a sort of stage-gate approval process where stakeholders sign off features. (This anti-pattern is typical of organizations using an agile-waterfall hybrid: Correctly, it is the prerogative of the product owner to decide what to ship and when.)
- **No stakeholders:** Stakeholders do not attend the sprint review. (There are several reasons why stakeholders do not go to the sprint review: They do not see any value in the ceremony. It conflicts with another important meeting. They do not understand the importance of the sprint planning event. No sponsor is participating in the sprint planning [like from the C-level]. In my experience, you need to "sell" the ceremony within the organization. This necessity is a topic the candidate should address with the scrum team.)
- **No customers:** External stakeholders – also known as customers – do not attend the sprint review. (Break out of

your organization's filter bubble, and invite some paying users of your product.)

- **Starting over again:** There is no continuity in the attendance of stakeholders. (Longevity is not just a team issue, it also applies to stakeholders. If they change too often, for example, because of a rotation scheme, how can they provide in-depth feedback? If this pattern appears, the team needs to improve how stakeholders understand the sprint review.)
- **Passive stakeholders:** The stakeholders are passive and unengaged. (This is simple to fix. Let the stakeholders drive the sprint review by putting them at the helm. Or, organize the sprint review as a science fair with several booths.)

There is one way, though, that a candidate can instantly contribute to the sprint review: at the end of it, run a quick and anonymous NPS-like poll (with a 1-10 scale on the value delivered by the last sprint) among all attendees. (You can prepare and print the forms in advance and bring them to the sprint review.)

If the product owner or the scrum team is not yet using such polls, the candidate can provide valuable insight to initiate further discussions on how to improve.

Less Suitable Topics for a Trial Day

A well-planned trial day provides about five hours of net collaboration time to enable the team to form an opinion on the candidate, and vice-versa. Given this limited time-box, and that you lack most of the context the team is working in, the options for practical work are limited. (Consider also that you have no social standing within the organization.)

Hence, there are a few topics where your opinion would be valuable to the organization, as well as your prospective teammates, and where you can spark or contribute to a discussion. Keep in mind that there will barely be enough time to sway an outcome.

The best you can do is prepare well for these topics and deliver some ideas about what you would do if given a chance to work with the team. The two most important issues are product discovery and agile metrics (with the latter one often reduced to velocity in practice).

Product Discovery

Product discovery is a great topic (not just for scrum masters) covering:

- How to realize dual-track agile or scrum within the organization,
- How to support the product owner in aligning product discovery with product delivery efforts,
- How to create, visualize, and prioritize hypotheses on what customers would consider valuable,
- How to run experiments to either validate or falsify those assumptions, and
- When to include the scrum team in the product discovery work.

In my experience, dual-track agile only works if everyone within the organization – management, stakeholders, product people, engineering, QA, and DevOps – is aligned with and fully supportive of the concept. And as a scrum master, you can substantially contribute to realizing this vision by coaching everyone involved. It is unfortunate that it is impossible to do so on a trial day.

Read More: "Product Discovery Anti-Patterns Leading to Failure."

Velocity and other Agile Metrics

Be prepared to answer some pertinent questions on velocity: What is your take on velocity? Do you consider it a valuable metric? Can you discuss any problems of the metric – maybe its inherent volatility, or the probable moral hazard in the form of estimate inflation?

The velocity discussion often seamlessly leads to both the idea behind flow and the #NoEstimates movement. Ask yourself, then, why on earth should we try to predict the future? (**Recommended video**: "#NoEstimates" by Allen Holub.)

Prepare an opinion on suitable agile metrics in general – and velocity in particular. Wrap your head around flow, cycle and lead time, and how all of this works (at a system thinking level) in conjunction with dual-track agile. (It would not make a lot of sense optimizing for product delivery when product discovery is lagging behind, would it? Remember that Scrum can also be great at efficiently delivering the wrong product.)

The positive aspect of the velocity/agile metric topic is that you can raise a lot of questions which are directed at the organization's path to becoming a learning organization. These issues can point beyond the usual application of scrum practices. A healthy discussion will also help you determine whether the organization is already agile, planning to become agile, or more likely to stay in the "doing agile" corner.

Read More: "Agile Metrics—The Good, the Bad, and the Ugly."

Wrap-up Session at the End of a Trial Day

There is usually a wrap-up session at the end of a trial day when the candidate shares their observations with the team. This wrap-up session can take anywhere between 15 to 60 minutes and may come in different formats and settings.

The format could be a time for more analysis when the candidate details their positive and negative observations and suggests areas for the team to work on. (A good team would return the favor and share their findings with the candidate.) Or the setting could be more casual as in a chat over coffee with the team – and probably some people from HR and management.

No matter in what format the wrap-up turns out to be, it is highly recommended that you should take notes throughout the trial day. Organizations, as well as prospective teammates, value attention to detail. You should not expect that you will be able to remember all the minutiae at the end of an exhausting day. Observations of "little things" from a fresh, unbiased mind will enable you to make astute and functional suggestions on how a team can improve. And this is at the heart of your value proposition to both the team and the organization.

PART V

APPENDIX

What is Next?

If you already have an offer on the table after your trial day, congratulations! With all the different variables that can influence your decision, I hope that this guide will help your deliberation be easy. (Make sure, though, that your remuneration is adequate and get your copy of The Scrum Master Salary Report 2017.)

If you like to get real-time support and feedback from thousands of your peers, consider joining the Hands-on Agile Slack community.

May I ask a favor of you? If this guide has proven itself to be helpful for your next career step, would you leave a review on Amazon or iBooks so other agile peers might learn from your experience? Your feedback would be much appreciated!

This is the review page for "How to Get Hired as a Scrum Master."

Please Review the Book and Help Your Peers to Find it!

If you like the book, please write a review — I am looking forward to learning about your feedback:

- Amazon reviews.
- iBooks review. (Not yet available as of January 9th, 2018.)

How to Get in Touch With Me

"Ship early, ship often." This practice will also apply to this book. I will regularly revise and expand it and also offer the latest version for my readers.

On top of that, I would like to recommend subscribing to the newsletter from "Age of Product," which I will use to be in constant contact with my readers.

If you would like to write to me privately, you can do so via email: stefan@age-of-product.com.

You can find me on Twitter — @StefanW and @AgeOfProduct — and LinkedIn.

Other Books for Agile Practitioners

'How to Get Hired as a Scrum Master' is a publication of a new series, providing hands-on advice on the everyday business of agile practitioners. Another available book is:

- "Lean User Testing" is a practical guide for everyone who wants to design, create or market software: product managers, developers, designers (UX/UI), entrepreneurs, as well as marketing and salespeople. Learn how to gain 80% of the insights of a professional UX agency by running user interviews yourself.

Printed in Poland
by Amazon Fulfillment
Poland Sp. z o.o., Wrocław